TERROR AT TENERIFE

by

George Otis

with

Norman Williams

Published by
Omega Publications
P.O. Box 4130
Medford, OR 97501

Cover design by Maurice T. Wagner.

Published by
Omega Publications
P.O. Box 4130
Medford, Oregon 97501

Printed in U.S.A.

ISBN 0-931-608-16-3
Omega #5116
Unilit #683641

FOREWORD

This writing is meant as a chronicle of memorable deeds by those aboard the big wounded birds and those who rushed to love them in a moment of crisis.

Stories of heroism, heartache and triumph were straining to be told, "His word was in my heart as a burning and I could not forbear telling of it." Tower personnel, medics and nurses, along with flight crews on both airliners wrote epistles of courage by their deeds.

A particular salute to Royal Dutch airlines and Pan American World Airways whose hearts ached so deeply. And to personnel of the entire airline industry we say, thank you for 50 years of dedication and safety.

George Otis

DEDICATION

Bob Stone, Jackie Mitchum, Ellen Zimmerman,
Richard Mann, Othella Williams,
Maurice Wagner and Norman — indispensable collaborators.

TABLE OF CONTENTS

CHAPTER ONE
Prelude to Disaster

The door of the plane slammed closed. The engines of our Pan American jumbo jet began to whine.

Looking past the two women on my left, framed in the window, I could see the green and white tail of the KLM 747 that had blocked our way while it had been refueling. It was turning slowly and moving out toward the main runway. Now, at last, I could feel the first tremors of our own movement. After some four hours of delay due to a whole series of events, we were on our way. About time, I thought . . .

Earlier we had flown five hours from Los Angeles to New York. Then, after an hour's stopover at Kennedy, we had been airborne another six hours to the Canary Islands. So, being cooped up in the plane for hours after landing at the Tenerife airport hadn't been any picnic. During these seemingly endless hours, we were only allowed to walk down the exit stairway and stand at the bottom of the steps for a "breather." Even the diversion of eating had come to an end—all that was left on board was coffee, soft drinks, peanuts. Some vacation!

We had touched down at Tenerife at 2:00 P.M. and now it was 6:00. There were 382 hungry, edgy passengers all just as anxious as I to fly those 40 minutes to Las Palmas on Grand Canary Island, our original destination. At Las Palmas we were to board the exquisite *M.S. Golden Odyssey* for a 12-day Mediterranean cruise.

You could hear a sigh of relief as our plane began to follow the KLM which was taxiing a half mile or so ahead toward the head of the runway for takeoff.

Why were we at Tenerife airport instead of Las Palmas where we were supposed to be? It was just one of the many events, stranger than fiction, which only destiny would dare to string together. Little things and not so little . . .

It was about a half hour before we were to land that the airliner's P.A. system came on. All passenger chatter quieted.

"Ladies and gentlemen, this is Captain Grubbs. We have just been instructed by Las Palmas control that we are to land instead at Tenerife which is only about 60 miles away. Apparently, there are some difficulties at the airport. But arrangements are being made to transfer you on to Las Palmas with a minimum of delay. As soon as we get more information, I will let you know."

The landing at Tenerife was just so-so. I had the feeling the airport was never designed with the 747 in mind. Captain Grubbs had to make use of every foot of that runway. The braking procedure seemed to me to be more sudden and intense.

The delay that ensued grew longer and longer and I thought how I would have loved to have taken a tour of Santa Cruz de Tenerife, instead of just waiting out the "difficulties." Finally we were told that there had been an explosion at Las Palmas. We were not told that the explosion was caused by a terrorist bombing, only that we were expecting clearance to go on to Las Palmas within the hour, so there would be no deplaning.

Then, after awhile, Captain Grubbs came back on the P.A. system. "Ladies and gentlemen, I have authorized the door to be opened and the stair ramp set in place so that any who wish can walk down and stretch their legs. Due to the number of other airliners here now because of the problem in

An inappropriate word considering who the author!

Las Palmas, we can't get near the terminal. In fact, the terminal facilities are already overloaded by other passengers. So remain close to our plane if you walk down the ramp. There are other planes alongside so we have to limit the number of disembarking persons, but everybody will get a little turn. I hope we can get you out of here in an hour or so."

I went twice. My business colleague, Ted Younes, joined me the first time. He was sitting directly in front of me on the aisle. Actually, it was due to Ted that I was taking the *Golden Odyssey* tour. He had made reservations for himself and his wife over a year ago. Then his wife changed her mind. Ted offered me her ticket. I had never seen the Mediterranean highlights we were to visit: Athens, Casablanca, Gibraltar. I accepted with great anticipation. Places I always dreamed of seeing.

The first time I stretched my legs outside I remarked to Ted how crowded the airport looked. There were five or six big airliners ahead of us and 11 or 12 behind us.

"Ted, it's going to take a lot more than an hour to untangle this mess," I said.

He grumbled, "It sure is."

It was windy. A huge mountain brooded over us, Pico de Teide—"The Peak of Hell." A volcano 12,000 feet high and ominous looking, the natives of Tenerife have many stories about this peak of hell looming out there in the Atlantic Ocean.

Back in the plane, our tour guide, Beau, was coming on the intercom every few minutes with welcome bits of information about boarding the big cruise ship once we landed at Las Palmas. Once he announced, "The *Golden Odyssey* will sail as soon as we are all aboard. The captain is holding a reception and a cocktail party starting at 7:00 P.M." There were cheers and the tension began to lift.

Beau kept coming "on the air" with pleasant pictures of what awaited us within an hour. "Each stateroom on the

Golden Odyssey is richly carpeted and handsomely furnished. You fancy folks from Leisure World will enjoy all the comforts of home. She is beautiful! Lots of drawer space, plenty of mirrors, airconditioning that can make you warmer or cooler. Your own private telephone with room service night and day. How's that?" There were 41 passengers aboard from Leisure World, a swank retirement city in Orange County, California.

But poor Beau's announcements got more and more sterile. They were interrupted every few minutes by Captain Grubbs' businesslike voice which itself radiated less and less patience. He had not relished the idea of waiting for the KLM plane to complete its refueling back where we had parked. He'd even thought we might squeeze around the refueling KLM and takeoff first, and sent his First Officer, Robert Bragg, to check it out.

The Captain was a gracious communicator. We never felt "left out." I got the impression that he was passing information on to us as fast as he was getting it himself:

- The explosion at Las Palmas.
- Reasons for the congestion here at Tenerife.
- The reopening over at Las Palmas.
- The scheduling of our takeoff.
- Then about the further delay because the refueling KLM was blocking our way out to the runway.
- Finally the closing of the doors and departure.

Copilot Bragg had left the plane and paced off the distance between the refueling KLM jet and the edge of the taxiway to see if there was room for our plane to ease through. Bad news, it was short less than 15 feet. It was to prove worlds away. That was when Grubbs' voice most betrayed his frustration. The Captain announced in clipped tones we would have to wait that extra half hour for the Dutch Captain van Zanten's refueling to be completed.

When I went down the stair ramp for my second stretch, daylight was beginning to wane. The wind was picking up and a large cloud on the "Peak of Hell" was slowly dropping. I shivered as I looked at it and felt the wind. Now, we Californians aren't strangers to fog . . .

"I hope we don't get fogged in here and have more delay," I remarked to an elderly passenger standing near me who was also looking up at that mountain.

"Could happen," he shrugged, as if time didn't make that much difference to him.

It did happen! Pico de Teide was dropping its shroud. Soon after I got back in my seat, wind-driven mist had enveloped the airport. At times you couldn't see the next plane. Then suddenly visibility would increase to a few hundred yards, and just as suddenly the white shroud would descend again.

I have trouble sitting for long stretches. My back was still aching from a recent operation. I had tried for a third stretch of my legs but a yellow rope had been placed across the door. Apparently, I was a little too late but a number of us stood by the door and just looked out at the thickening fog being swept downward by the wind. Departure was announced and I returned to my seat.

"It's like pea soup," the elderly woman next to me remarked to her daughter by the window, as our plane began to move.

"Don't worry, mother," she replied. "Remember how thick the fog was when we took off in Fort Lauderdale. This is all perfectly safe. They have radar and lots of equipment. Pilots always do things right."

What we didn't know was that there was no ground radar at all. A few months before, Spanish air controllers at the Tenerife airport had staged a slowdown protesting the antiquated radar equipment and undermanned facilities. Tenerife airport had been the subject of continuing aviation news relative to its safety problems.

Due to the mountain fog that repeatedly blankets this field, a safer airport was being built to replace it at Santa Cruz. It had been started several years before and the runways were completed, but that was all.

Our plane trundled slowly along, following the same taxiing path that the KLM plane had taken a couple of minutes earlier.

No use trying to look out the window—fog, fog, fog. I hitched my seat belt and settled back comfortably.

Meanwhile, communications were going on between the tower and the pilots of both planes. With no ground radar the Tower's control function depended solely on radio voice contact.

Tower Control instructed Captain van Zanten in the KLM plane: "Taxi the full length of Runway 30, make a 180 degree turn and hold."

To our Captain Grubbs: "Follow KLM about three minutes behind and turn off at third intersection."

Ordinary procedure would have been for both planes to use the access taxiway to reach the takeoff point at the end of the runway. But this was clogged by all the flights re-routed here because of the terrorist bombing over at Las Palmas.

So we both had to taxi right up the main 11,000 foot runway. Then our plane was to pull off at the third access ramp until KLM took off. After that we were to proceed back out on the main runway, taxi to the end and prepare for takeoff.

These conversations between pilots and Tower Control are, of course, not heard by the passengers. I was lost in the usual kinds of thoughts that we all indulge in, reviewing the day's events, anticipating the cruise to follow.

It was now about 6:00 P.M., Canary Islands time—back home in Rancho Palos Verdes, California, about noon. It had been 24 hours since my mother and I had said our good-byes. After my father's death in 1959, my mother chose to make her home with me. She maintains the home for me, as I am a bachelor and have never married. Other vital statistics: I am 52, six feet tall and weigh about 250 pounds, too heavy and out of shape. My mother, Othella Williams, is in her 70s, young looking, and has lots of energy.

Right about now she would be making herself some lunch. I hoped she wasn't worrying. I travel a lot, both on business and for pleasure. Just yesterday, we had lunch together. I packed, made some phone calls, then it was time to leave for the airport.

"Norman, let's pray together." My mother went over to the book shelves and pulled out the Bible. We both put our hands on the Bible and prayed for my safe return. She cried. Never before had she cried when we prayed before a trip.

As I thought about that now, while the plane continued its fog-enshrouded movement along the runway, it struck me that although we frequently prayed together, this was the first time that we prayed so fervently before a trip.

Then my thoughts wandered back to the California College of Commerce of which I am president. Able administrators keep things running smoothly so my presence isn't essential. Even though Ted, our administrator, was with me here on the airliner we had no concerns in our both being away.

Ted and I also shared an interest in real estate investing. In fact, he was studying for his real estate license. I leaned sideways in my chair to see if Ted had the study material he had brought along to bone up for the licensing exam but he, too, appeared to be relaxing and watching the fog go by the windows.

I glanced out my window. Fog—lots of it. There was still a chance we could get socked in before we got clearance for takeoff. In Tenerife the airport could be open one minute, closed the next. The fog came and went. At the moment, it had really come. I wondered how the KLM could ever see.

In 40 minutes we should be at Las Palmas. Originally, a

bus tour of Grand Canary Island had been scheduled before boarding the ship. But this delay at Tenerife had used up our sightseeing time. I hoped that on the way back we would be able to re-schedule that. I certainly had not seen anything of the Canary Islands so far—except an overloaded airport and the Peak of Hell.

Baggage. It would be easy in Las Palmas. I only had a garment bag and a carry-on case. The stewardess had hung my garment bag in the forward closet. The carry-on case was under the seat in front of me.

Meanwhile up on the flight decks both planes were chattering with Tower Control.

KLM #4806 up the runway requested, "Confirm Pan Am moving off runway at third exit ramp."

"Affirmative," replied Tower Control. "One, two, three. The third one, sir."

Captain Victor Grubbs was moving our Pan Am "Clipper Victor," at only six miles per hour due to the heavy ground fog. Normal taxi speed would have been more like 20 miles an hour.

Captain Grubbs turned to Copilot Robert Bragg. "This field is below takeoff minimum. When we get to the end of the runway, we are going to hold off until the weather improves."

Meanwhile, he was counting exit ramps. His instructions were to exit at the third. He did not count the first because it was clogged with standby planes. The first clear exit ramp was meant for entrance, not exit. It required a sharp turn, more than 90 degrees and would head him back into the terminal.

The next ramp was exactly the same—dangerously narrow and at an awkward angle for an exit. He called this number two and headed for the third. He could see about 500 feet ahead through momentary breaks in the fog that this one was angled better and was the one he was to take.

KLM to Tower Control: "Request air control clearance."

This was not a request to takeoff but the standard request for the flight path that the plane is to take after it would get airborne. Control Tower then gave the KLM plane those airplane flight details: "To Papa Beacon, climb to 9,000, right turn to heading 040 until intercept 325 radial."

KLM repeated them and radioed the Tower: "We are now at takeoff."

Tower Control to KLM jet: "Stand by for takeoff clearance. I will call you back."

Captain Grubbs confirmed this to our Copilot Bragg. "He's not cleared for takeoff."

Tower Control, having put the KLM airliner on hold, was now interested in knowing when our Pan Am jumbo was exiting so that the go ahead for takeoff could be given the KLM when the visibility permitted.

Tower Control to Pan Am: "Clipper 1736, report clear of runway."

Pan Am to Tower Control: "Will report when clear of runway."

Tower Control to Pan Am: "Roger, thank you."

But the communications I was hearing was between a mother and daughter, my seatmates in 29A and 29B.

"I need another double scotch as soon as they start serving. My arthritis is killing me. I wish they'd do it now."

"I don't know what they are waiting for. I'm ready for one too."

These two women had been on "doubles" all the way from Los Angeles. They rationalized they needed that "anesthetic" for their pain. The mother was 88, the daugher 62. I am equally sure that for most of the trip they were stoned. Sitting on the aisle, I was kept busy shuttling the refills and empties back and forth.

I put my head back against the upholstered seat, closed my eyes and relaxed.

Our Captain stiffened as he peered through the mist. Lights on the runway ahead! Were they moving toward us or standing still? The fog blurred them.

Copilot Bragg leaned forward and screamed, "He's moving!"

The Pan Am radio had been on continuously. The pilots of each jet could hear each other as they talked back and forth with the tower.

Captain Grubbs shouted into his microphone: "We're still on the runway!" Then our Copilot . . . "What's he doing—he'll kill us all!"

Copilot Bragg shouted to Captain Grubbs to take escape action by getting off the runway: "Get off! Get off!"

The giant KLM 747, named "the Rhine," thundered under full power right at us.

Captain Grubbs gunned his engines and veered sharply to the left, attempting to get it off the runway, in a desperate maneuver to avoid being struck.

I felt a bump and a drop as one set of our wheels left the runway. It wasn't far enough.

I felt the sudden jerk of the plane to the left and still another slump downward. Another wheel left the runway. I didn't know what was happening.

Meanwhile in the cockpit of the big airliner there was brilliant Captain Veldhuyzen van Zanten, KLM's top pilot. He served as the number one jet instructor on the airline of the dependable Dutch service. But during the past 60 minutes he had behaved out of character. In Captain van Zanten's haste to get back home he had taken on 142,000 pounds of extra jet fuel so he wouldn't have to be delayed again when he disgorged his passengers over at Las Palmas. This great extra weight would make his jet that much more sluggish at liftoff.

Now the normally careful Captain was in such a hurry

he was trying to leave Tenerife with miserable visibility and another airliner somewhere down that same runway trying to find an exit ramp. Suddenly the Dutchman spotted through the wind-driven fog the ghostly outline of another big airplane still partially on his runway with its powerful forward lights piercing the mist.

At full takeoff power van Zanten was already rolling at nearly 180 miles per hour. In that split second he must have remembered the 142,000 unnecessary extra pounds of jet fuel. But too late. Only one chance—try to pull his sluggish ship up over the Pan Am. Van Zanten pulled the control yoke clear back into the pit of his stomach and heard his own tail gouging a furrow in the Tenerife runway. She would hardly fly, 142,000 pounds too heavy and by now the blue and white Pan Am looked like it was already inside his own cockpit.

Van Zanten frantically shouted, *"Gott dam!"* But the problem which was in the making wasn't God's doing.

Some passengers on the right side of our own plane knew what was coming. They could see the KLM plane approaching. But until the last second it looked like an apparition that would go away. Then too late they knew it wasn't a dream but 300 tons of flying aluminum, steel and fuel. "We're going to crash! We've got to get out of here!" a San Francisco man yelled to his wife.

"The KLM is taking off on our runway!" another screamed.

When I first felt the wheel slump downward the impact came in seconds and I thought that whatever was happening to our plane must be as a result of that ditch into which the wheel seemed to drop.

There was instant fire.

Explosion.

Screams.

Havoc.

I was on my feet. I don't remember unbuckling my seat belt.

Searing flames blasted through the cabin. Fragments of white, hot metal shot in my face.

My first impulse was to help the old lady next to me. But she was not in her seat. Just gone. She and her daughter had collapsed downward as if into the floor, buried under debris.

Heartrending shouts for husbands or wives filled the air, intermixed with the smashing sounds of destruction and the roaring of fire. And cursing . . . such cursing! Everything was fire, smoke, shrapnel and tumult.

My next reaction was to turn to my partner Ted in the seat ahead of me. But Ted was not there—simply gone.

Then another explosion wracked the plane. A lightning-like sheet of flame cremated human flesh and metal alike—front to back—vaporizing everything in its path.

Through the flames a huge object came hurtling directly at me. It was white hot. I threw up my arms in an automatic reflex. I felt unexplainably strong. It struck my arms and was deflected. I don't know what it was. How could I have stopped that huge object?

Within these first few seconds after impact everybody in the seats behind me with but one or two exceptions were already dead. The exploding KLM had rammed right through. I did not even know the KLM plane had hit us. Its captain trying to liftoff, hoping to leap frog over us, it had roared toward us at 180 miles per hour—a giant bomb filled with good people and fuel.

The nose of the KLM plane cleared our Pan Am but the fuselage of the Dutch jet ripped us midsection. KLM's number three engine took off our entire upper lounge behind the cockpit. Their wing sliced off the bubble. Number four engine passed in front of our cockpit.

Fragments of our plane were sucked into its 2,000 degrees Fahrenheit engines as the KLM slammed down, skidded around, slipped backward for 1,500 feet, before exploding into a molten mass. None of those dear Dutch survived a minute.

As one of our passengers, Bethene Moore, later described, "I had been leaning down arranging some carry-on luggage under the seat in front of me when the whole side of the plane came in. The other plane's wing came across and our top was completely sheared off. Instantly I could see the sky above me." *or the fog?*

Jim Novik, a travel agent with the booking firm in San Francisco that chartered our flight, was sitting in the first-class compartment. He later said, "I heard an explosion. The ceiling caved in. A piece of the ceiling fell on my wife as I was trying to unfasten her seat belt. Then there was another terrible explosion. It threw her out of the plane. I jumped, too, just as the flames came."

But there was no escaping the flames that engulfed me. Yet, I was not burned. Others melted down into blackened corpses in these few seconds following the impact. They seemed immobilized. Frozen with shock. They just sat there docilely and died.

But I wasn't ready for that yet and decided to get on the move. To where or how I didn't know . . .

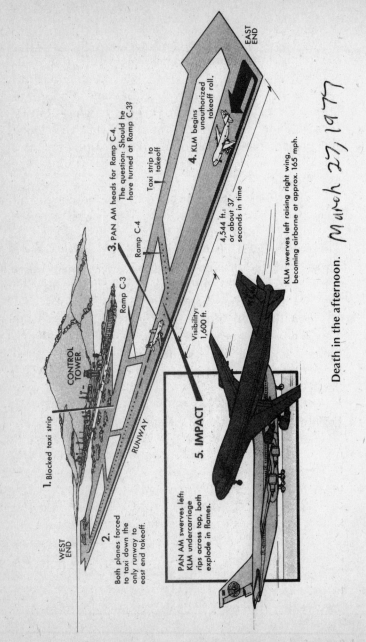

1. Blocked taxi strip

WEST END

CONTROL TOWER

Ramp C-3

RUNWAY

Ramp C-4

2. Both planes forced to taxi down the only runway to east end takeoff.

3. PAN AM heads for Ramp C-4. The question: Should he have turned at Ramp C-3?

Taxi strip to takeoff

4. KLM begins unauthorized takeoff roll.

EAST END

Visibility: 1,600 ft.

4,544 ft.: or about 37 seconds in time

KLM swerves left raising right wing, becoming airborne at approx. 165 mph.

5. IMPACT

PAN AM swerves left: KLM undercarriage rips across top, both explode in flames.

March 27, 1977

Death in the afternoon.

TIME diagram by Don Mackay

CHAPTER TWO
Killed Five Times

Meanwhile Paul and Floy Heck of Leisure World were sitting in seats 34D and 34E. Paul was a JPL purchasing agent and proud of being a member of the High Flyers. Floy is a coloratura soprano who sang in the White House. The Hecks were on the flight with their friends sitting in 34F and 34G.

They said, "We met our friends Carl and Lorraine Larson in October of 1976 on a Caribbean cruise. We became immediate close friends. Since they were going on the *Golden Odyssey* Mediterranean cruise they urged us to go with them. It was also through their influence that we moved to Leisure World. Great people!

"We always have daily devotions and so before leaving on this vacation tour I had knelt, praying, 'Father, Your will be done.' I always prayed that way and then we were never unhappy over a trip. 'Keep us safe on land, sea or in the air.' I continued, 'Father, when we return we will kneel in this same spot here in our bedroom and both give You thanks.' "

Paul said, "After my return three weeks later from the hospital I looked at Floy as we entered the door and said, 'Honey, we have something to do.' We went to our bedroom to the exact spot giving thanks to God for His faithfulness."

Then he retraced their experiences at Tenerife airport.

"We were sitting in the plane when we heard a terrible explosion. Someone screamed, 'It's a bomb!' I heard ripping metal—front to right. I turned to my wife and yelled, 'Honey, get your seat belt off. Come on!' She released her belt and immediately as I turned I felt her presence behind me. I looked up and saw the ceiling was falling down, the jet fuel had ruptured from the other plane and was streaming in. Our seats were right behind the wing and as I gazed to the left I saw an opening and we crawled out on the wing.

"I thought Floy was still behind me and stumbled to the end of the wing tip. At that moment my greatest fear was falling into the jet engines that were still on. Captain Grubbs never got a chance to shut them down. I realized I could be sucked right into the jet. When I saw the 20 foot jump beneath me I looked back and Floy was gone. She had vanished. I looked down again and thought, 'If I jump I'll break my legs and be unable to get away from the wreck. I'll be trapped under the wing.' Then a miracle happened. I'll never forget it. Clearly I heard, 'Though he fall, he shall not be utterly cast down: for the Lord upholdeth him with his hand.' Later I was to find it's a piece of the 37th Psalm. I knew I could jump and somehow not be utterly cast down, even as I hit the hard runway surface far below.

"I jumped. I was badly hurt but I could still move. My back was sprained, my head was cut open. My hands had been terribly cooked as I pushed away columns of fire when Floy and I had fought our way out onto the wing. I knew I had to get away from there. I knew I was now in a desperate situation because I was under the fuel-filled wing and maybe in more danger than before. It would blow any minute.

"I crawled furiously. Then I heard the explosion. Now burning metal was flying over me and beyond me. I knew there was terrible danger of a third cataclysmic explosion. I clawed away in the dirt, praying, 'God save my wife. You say all things are possible. Give me strength to crawl away from the wreck.' The third explosion thundered behind me. Finally I knew I was safe because the debris was falling behind me. I looked down the runway. Rubble was everywhere. KLM a distant fiery mountain of metal.

"Two Tenerife men came and lifted me. They were so shaken themselves that their knees knocked—I could see them. Their teeth chattered—I could hear them. I wondered, 'Who is holding up who?' Oh, they were so brave.

"I was in such terrible pain and now found I had another problem—nobody could understand my cries for relief. The pain was indescribable. Finally, I held up my scorched and bloody hands saying, 'Morphine.' Evidently a man there at the First Aid station was a medic. He understood and gave me a shot. Then two Tenerife men loaded me into a taxi which originally had brought me to the First Aid station. They took me for a hair-raising ride. It was almost humorous as I mused, 'I've escaped the plane crash—now I'm going to be killed in a taxi.'

"I recalled the other injured I had seen. Clothes blown off, moaning, broken legs, shattered hips, burns. My greatest anxiety at this point was that I had failed my wife. It tortured me. Poor Floy. I had known she was behind me when we got out of the wreck. But where had she gone? She had just vanished. It gave me more pain than my burns. I got her out onto the wing but at the last moment had I failed? Had I left Floy behind? From the experience—when I later learned my wife was safe, I've appreciated Floy much more than ever before. She's nearer and dearer and more valuable to me. It was like getting Floy back from the dead."

Paul Heck recalled how immediately on impact he had turned and looked for his Leisure World friends, Lorraine and Karl. "But they sat there looking stunned—in the end they just sat there and perished. However, Floy and I recall how often Lorraine would say, "Whenever and however Karl goes to be with the Lord, I want to go too.' They did. They went together—side by side." Paul saw others patiently sitting there in the plane "immobile and glassy-eyed like rows of figures in a wax museum."

When we asked Paul Heck what he recalls hearing in the final minute in the wreck he said, "Please don't ever ask me that. I will never even tell my wife. There are those who had loved ones and it would not be right to leave them with any lingering memories."

"I couldn't help but reflect on the strange saga of my own string of survivals. I hope this doesn't bore you but:

"*Fire:* Saved from a burning theater as a boy of 8.

"*Explosion:* Worked with explosives in construction. On impulse a crazy fellow-worker picked up a full box of unstable explosives and threw them up in the air. 'This is it,' I thought. No one ever could explain this but the nitro never exploded.

"*Crush and cut:* As a machinist a huge cutter blade (with 50 tons of pressure) flew off. If I had followed the natural instinct to jump back I would have been killed. Standing motionless my cap was knocked off and the back of my shirt torn to shreds.

"*Electrocution:* As night foreman I was called upon to fix a huge machine. I threw the high voltage line switch and turned it off at the fuse box. When another machinist came out of the washroom he saw it was off and turned the power back on again. I was immediately struck with this intensive power and thrown back alive!

"*Holocaust:* Finally the terror at Tenerife and more alive than ever. Praise God for His protective angels! He has sent one to save my life again. Five times in all."

Floy Heck said, "At the crash it was Hell on earth. Then I went into a kind of a silent world. Stunned and frozen in my seat I thought, 'This is it.' You may ask me, 'Were you praying, were you frightened, were you thinking of your children?' No! I was frozen stiff with shock.

"Then I heard my husband command, 'Floy, come on! Come on!' I instantly obeyed and followed him out onto the wing. He actually pushed a shimmering column of fire aside burning his hands severely and crawled on ahead of me to the very end of the tilted-up wing. I thought to myself, 'Why is Paul going to the highest part of the wing to jump?' Of course, I never realized a person could be sucked into those still screaming jet engines.

"God played a great part in my escape here as He knew that my brittle bones could never withstand the still higher jump I would have to make from way out on the wing tip. I looked down and saw two women dive head first right through the emergency door—like graceful high divers fully clothed. I wondered why they would go head first. I stepped out onto the wide fairing at the wing root and jumped.

"It was a fearsome height but I landed on something. When I looked it was a man. Those other two had dived on him and he just lay their motionless. I knew he was dead. He had escaped the wreck only to die. Then I blacked out. I had struck my head.

"When I came to I was thinking, 'My legs hurt, I can't move,' but I knew the whole airplane was ready to blow up. Somehow I had to get away. I started praying, 'Dear Jesus, help me, help us, help everyone, oh, bless these dear people.' I started crawling and kept praying. Then I remembered— polyester clothes! They were so flammable. Why hadn't I burned already?

"I heard a third explosion. I turned. Now the whole plane was on fire. Several months before we had seen the movie *Hindenburg*. I thought, 'This looks just like the burning—the dirigible. Where is my husband—why is he neglecting me?' Strange thoughts. Paul had already gotten me out. I saw all the people lying on the grass. I thought they were just some kind of spectators. Semi-delirious reasoning. I saw others in great pain and such anguish. Cries of, 'I am losing my leg. I'll never walk again! I'm bleeding to death.'

"Someone said, 'Let's pray!' They were praying the Lord's prayer. Wonderful thought. Now, I was praying loudest of them all. I was in such shock when I arrived at the hospital. Shaking head to toe I spoke in my faltering Spanish, 'Mucho-free-O, Mucho-free-O.' (Cold! Cold!) Again I asked them, 'Pablo Heck? Pablo Heck?'

"No one knew. Later they were to get Paul on the phone for me. They found him alive over at the Residence Hospital in Tenerife. But that's another miracle.

"When I arrived in my room I was again to Praise God for they had put me in with a Charismatic Christian lady who had both arms bound. Through the night I would hear Erma Schlecht softly praying. I asked, 'Erma, are you hurting?' She would say, 'Yes, Floy.' Then we would both go to prayer. It was better than the medicine. Thanks, Erma.

"You ask me, 'Will we ever be the same again?' Oh, I hope not! Of course we won't—we don't want to be. We want to be better for these experiences.

"Will we need a psychiatrist? No! Although we faced death we have no nightmares. The Bible says, 'All those who know you Lord will count on you for help.'

"Physical suffering: 'But the God of all grace, who hath called us unto his eternal glory by Christ Jesus, after that ye have suffered a while, make you perfect, stablish, strengthen, settle you' (1 Peter 5:10).

"Why do some perish and others live? 'O the depth of the riches both of the wisdom and knowledge of God! how unsearchable are his judgments, and his ways past finding out! For who hath known the mind of the Lord? or who hath been his counselor? Or who hath first given to him, and it shall be recompensed unto him again? For of him, and through him, and to him, are all things: to whom be glory forever. Amen' (Romans 11:33).

"The Bible has come alive for us so much more.

"But I dreaded seeing Lorraine Larson's father. He lived alone in Torrance, California. I wondered what I could ever say to him. How could I console him? She was his only child. He called and asked if he could visit us. When he arrived he was so cheerful and said, 'Floy, Lorraine and Karl were both ready to be with God.' ''

Paul and Floy Heck,
Laguna Hills, Calif.

Photo by Diane Corder

The KLM 747 just blew up.
None survived.

Photo: Agence Sygma

CHAPTER THREE
The Road to Tenerife

. . . Still in the wreckage, I was groping through the inferno looking for a way out.

Most people died where they sat. If it did not happen in the first second, it happened the second, third or fourth . . . many just seemed to wait for it to happen.

Some stood in the aisles as if they were just watching all of this happen and were not really in there themselves. It did not appear to me that all were immobilized by fear. It seemed as if they were transfixed, like they just didn't care.

I cared. But my caring somehow did not trigger horror, panic or fear. And believe me, there was ample grounds for all three.

One second—joyous relief that after hours of tedious delay we were on our way and would soon board the *Golden Odyssey* cruise ship. The next second—an exploding inferno with people decapitated and incinerated along with the beautiful airplane that was twisting itself into a coffin.

There are grounds for horror in seeing people crumple into corpses and in hearing the sounds they make on the way down.

There are grounds for panic when roaring flames envelop you and flying metal slashes at you.

There are grounds for fear in knowing that next second may be your last.

Yet, I felt no panic, no fear. It was amazing.

My decision to move toward safety was made in quite the opposite mental climate. I felt a total clarity. I felt I was in good hands, and I don't mean some insurance company. Not really *deciding* to move but *agreeing* to move as a gentle nudge pressed me along.

This mental climate was not synthesized by me on the spot. It came when it was needed because of past mental postures.

I believe this "mental climate" can come to anybody who prepares for it and it can also be their "escape hatch" in times of crisis as it was for me.

"Mental climate"—"Escape hatch"? I think back to those years when I first became aware of it and when it first began to develop. Why, you can start today and survive a crisis if it should come tomorrow. It will work for every person who cares.

To better understand what was happening as I began to move in that fire it may be necessary to go back a moment over certain aspects of my life. As surely as we are breathing they prepared the way for my escaping this hellish inferno.

ROOTS

Strangely my father had experienced another kind of "inferno." It happened back in 1925 near Moberly, Missouri where on April 7 of that year I was born.

My grandfather owned a coal mine. One day he and my father were inspecting a vein of coal down in that mine. There was a sudden slide and my father was pinned under a huge boulder. That was a very dark "inferno."

My grandfather had to leave him alone and dying down there while he tried to get help. Yes, my father was not only cold and in darkness but he was all alone down in that mine. He could be buried by another slide any minute. The coal dust filtered down on him continuously.

When they finally got him out of there, they didn't

think he was going to live. He was alive but in agony. They rushed him to a hospital where the doctors found he had a broken back. That was enough to kill anyone in those days. If that weren't enough, ten broken ribs, a broken collar bone and brutal internal injuries were added to the list.

When the doctors gave my mother the news, she could hear what they were really saying, "Hopeless."

"Have you set his broken bones?"

"It would be too great a risk in his critical state. Now you understand the situation, Mrs. Williams?"

The doctors were without hope. But my mother wasn't without hope. Nor was my father without hope. My mother dug in and believed God meant for his recovery. It might be hopeless for the doctors but not for God. Dad was on the razor's edge but he made it. He confounded the doctors. Weeks later, he left the hospital.

Of course, by that time it was a bit late to reset the bones and he went through the rest of his life with periods of pain, but he was pulsing with life. It gave my mother plenty of practice being a nurse, a skill that she was to use to advantage for her four children, especially me. My father never went back into the mines. Several years later, we moved to Detroit and he began to develop his mechanical skills eventually becoming a top mechanic at Chrysler.

My parents had been only occasional churchgoers in Missouri, but with my father a living testimonial of God's miracle rescue, mother encouraged us to begin attending Brightmoor Tabernacle regularly. That was 1929. My religious and academic education got started early. I considered them about equal in my life as I grew, and religious education seemed every bit as important to survival in this world as the three "R's."

As a little boy, I remember the bread lines. Beggars were common. Father's mechanical skills enabled us to cope. So did the "skills" of our heavenly Father. You needed both in the depression.

In 1932, the family, all in one week, dedicated their lives to Jesus Christ as personal Savior. I was seven years old. At that age, it is usually not really appreciated. Some might suppose that a seven-year-old is just doing what his parents have asked him to do. But I remember it differently—it was a very special feeling. I was participating—experiencing, and something "clicked" deep inside my young heart.

This became evident as the years went by. At the age of 12 (I remember the date: December 12, 1937), it was my joyous experience to receive the baptism of the Holy Spirit. The power of the Holy Spirit moved in a new dimension within me.

Detroit life was big city life at its best and worst. Detroit had its advantages, which I enjoyed, but it also had its shabbiness and violence.

I left school at the age of 14 to work full time to help the family. Later I took the necessary examination to obtain my high school certificate. At 18 I entered Bible college.

There was a call of God on my life. That year, 1943, I enrolled as a student in Central Bible College, Springfield, Missouri. I graduated in 1946, receiving my diploma and became a licensed minister. For the next few years I helped pioneer a few churches in southern Missouri, Pennsylvania and Ohio.

I remember saying good-bye to the college dean. "I haven't been one of your best students. I only wish I would have done better."

He paused a moment as he shook my hand, "Norman, I'm not a gambling man, but if I were, I'd bet on you." It was a real encouragement but still I didn't know what I was going to do with my life.

That degree really felt good to me but there were aspects of my life I was not too secure about.

When I returned home to the family back in Detroit I discussed this uncertainty with them. It was my father who brought it up.

"There's not money in church work, Son."

"I know. But you get rich in other ways."

"How's this going to get you a meal ticket today? Things are real bad, Norman."

"God takes care of His own. I'll get by."

I broke the news to the family one night at dinner. "I'm going to enroll at the Detroit Business Institute. It will help me from becoming dependent on some church."

"Great!" my father responded. "I'll stake you the tuition."

Mother's reaction was less enthusiastic. "Go ahead, Norman, but don't ever forget your dedication to the Lord's work."

"That's impossible," I assured her. But it was possible, just as she feared.

My progress at the Detroit Business Institute was impressive. Soon I expanded my original program and swept on to advanced courses.

In a year or so—December, 1951—I moved to Los Angeles and transferred to a division of the Sawyer Schools for Business to complete my studies. Their business courses were somehow a natural for me. The director offered me a teaching job and I accepted enthusiastically.

My employer had a chain of business schools. He gave me an opportunity to invest in two of the schools. That was in 1959, the year my father died from a sudden heart attack. My mother decided to move from Detroit to Los Angeles and to make her home with me. With father gone and mother with me, financial security seemed all the more a priority.

As busy as I became, prayer and the study of God's Word remained a way of life. I studied the Bible several times over and prayer continued being a living thing with me. Not just in church, but in business and any place I might go. This may come as a surprise to some of my college associates, since I didn't "go public" with my devotion. I felt it was a personal thing. So they never saw me walking the corridors with a Bible in my hand. Maybe they should have.

Good habits are hard to break, too. Admittedly, the original dream faded, but devotion to the Lord remained a vital reality, and would prove one day to save my life.

However, there were private counseling sessions with students when a critical problem gave me a good excuse for asking God's help. Then pray we did—college or not. I remember once working with a troubled student. I said to him, "Arthur, intemperance can threaten not only your business career, but your life. The business words we work with here every day are never going to help in crisis. But there is one Word that can help. Are you interested?"

"Of course. What word?"

"The Word of God. Have you ever read the Bible?"

Arthur shrugged. "Not for years. Even then, I never took it seriously."

"Try again," I urged. "God can help you. Arthur, would you take a minute to pray with me?" This took him by surprise. We closed our eyes and bowed our heads. "In Jesus' name. Amen," I prayed.

Arthur was ready. His life changed, his studies improved and he went on to become a CPA.

I should have given more of myself, spiritually, than I did. I certainly felt frustration in cases where problems weren't solved. Like Karen's . . .

"There's no way. No way." Her voice was as expressionless as her face. She seemed empty. A fellow student had heard her talk about suicide. He rushed to me, and I called Karen into my office.

"There is always a way for those who dare to have faith." I watched for a reaction to that last word. There wasn't any. I must have sounded like empty wind.

She said, "There is just no reason for me to live. I can't go on."

I wished she would cry or something. She was emotionless. I won't go into the problem that brought her to this suicidal state. But whatever the problem, God had a solution for it.

"Have you prayed for help?"

"Oh, please, not that."

There was no reaching her. She would not pray. I needed time. It was Friday afternoon.

"Will you promise me something?"

She said, "What is it?"

"Promise me that you will be back here Monday morning. We'll work this out together. Everything will turn out." Time would help, I thought.

She hesitated, then said, "All right."

She kept her promise. She attended classes on Monday. When I saw her, I gave her a big smile. She never smiled back. It put me off—I wasn't sensitive to the depths of her trouble.

That night she killed herself.

Looking back, there were times when counseling didn't work. It should have been a closer, warmer relationship. After all, when you are explaining the computation of investment credits on straight line depreciation you are thinking more of the word of the Internal Revenue Service than the Word of God. It was, however, a day-by-day communication. There were changes for the better in some lives and a few problems were solved. The form of Godliness that I had in those years was not ministerial in degree, but it was nevertheless there.

I prayed with individual students, and sometimes with individual staff members when I could work the time in. The staff knew where I stood spiritually and we maintained good ethics and standards. I have always felt a strong consciousness of God and I consider it natural to call upon Him, not an abnormal thing that happens only in moments of crises or threat to survival. As hectic as the business could be at times, it never eclipsed my relationship with God.

It took this Tenerife cataclysm to show me I was not

"playing church." The work of this catastrophe may have to do with a real deepening of my relationship with God I did not realize I needed.

I am going to take you, my readers, back into that dying Pan Am jumbo jet and give you a microscopic view of what took place in my escape. But the end product of that trauma was its most important work. You can *feel* close to God when you pray daily as I was doing in the pre-Tenerife, serene days. You can feel close to God when you read the Bible. You feel close to God when you attend church and when you share with others. Through the years I have attended the Assemblies of God, although I do not belong to any one church. My sister and her family go to the Full Gospel Assembly in Bell Gardens, California. So, my mother and I attend that church quite regularly.

But I know now that no matter how close you feel to God, you can get vastly closer. You can indeed *be* closer. I'm closer today than before that violent March day and I intend to move closer still.

Though president of a college, I do not have to be there every day. The staff is highly skilled and responsible and there's no need for me to intervene continually. So when my colleague, Ted Younes, approached me about joining him on a Mediterranean cruise, I was open to the idea.

He handed me the brochures detailing the air-sea itinerary.

"Looks good, Ted, let me think it over. I'll talk to you tomorrow."

I pulled out the beautiful tour material after dinner and started reading aloud, "Ancient walled cities rising from the sea. Huge fortresses laced with winding cobblestone streets. Timeless monument of lost civilizations . . . " My mother put down her book to listen.

She interrupted, "You're not going to invest in that kind of real estate, I hope."

"No. I wish I did own it though. It's in the Mediterranean. I'm thinking of joining Ted Younes on a two week air-sea cruise. Tell you more about it when I get through these brochures."

After wading through the glowing testimonials, color photos and other public relations chatter, I got into the heart of the matter—the itinerary:

AIR FLIGHT #B206		ARRIVE	DEPART
March			
Sat.	26 Los Angeles		4:45 P.M.
Sun.	27 New York (JFK)	12:20 A.M.	1:45 A.M.
Sun.	27 Las Palmas	1:15 P.M.	

SHIP SCHEDULE

		ARRIVE	DEPART
March			
Sun.	27 Las Palmas		5:00 P.M.
Mon.	28 Funchal	8:00 A.M.	6:00 P.M.
Tues.	29 At Sea		
Wed.	30 Casablanca	8:00 A.M.	7:00 P.M.
Thurs.	31 Tangier	8:00 A.M.	1:00 P.M.
Thurs.	31 Gibraltar	4:00 P.M.	10:00 P.M.
April			
Fri.	1 At Sea		
Sat.	2 Palma	8:00 A.M.	7:00 P.M.
Sun.	3 At Sea		
Mon.	4 Valletta	8:00 A.M.	10:00 P.M.
Tues.	5 Messina	8:00 A.M.	10:00 P.M.
Wed.	6 At Sea		
Thurs.	7 Heraklion	8:00 P.M.	1:00 P.M.
Thurs.	7 Santorini	Sail through	
Fri.	8 Athens	7:00 A.M.	

AIR FLIGHT #B207

		April		
Fri.	8	Athens		8:30 P.M.
Sat.	9	New York (JFK)	3:20 A.M.	4:20 A.M.
Sat.	9	Los Angeles	7:00 A.M.	

All times local

Athens alone would be worth the whole trip. I decided to go, "Mother, I'm going."

Mother is a religious person but we do not have any daily rituals together. In a way she does her thing and I do mine. After all, she had already done what she could with me. She still reads the Bible regularly, in private. But at times, she brings the Bible over and we talk about particular discoveries together. It might be my imagination but, thinking back now, I have the feeling that in the month that followed before I departed, these moments of Bible sharing greatly increased.

I share this picture of my mother so you can place into perspective with what is now about to happen.

On Saturday, March 26, the day of departure, Mother and I had lunch together. When we finished, she looked at her watch.

"I guess it is about time for you to be leaving—there may be traffic."

I looked at my watch. The plane was scheduled to leave at 5:30 P.M. but we had been advised to be at the airport one hour early. The drive to LAX is about an hour.

"Yes," I replied, "better play it safe."

"All packed?"

"Ready to roll."

"Let's pray."

Mother went over to get the Bible. I placed my hands on the Book with hers.

"Lord, take care of us," she began. She prayed for a safe journey and a safe return.

There was a quality I had never heard in her voice. I raised my head to look at her. Tears were streaming down her face. I put my arm around her and asked God to be with her and to also keep her until my return.

It was natural of Mother to pray whenever I went on a trip. On a driving trip, she would walk around the car praying that God would keep His hand on the wheel. But I never saw Mother's tears while in prayer.

When you are tight for time the plane always seems to leave right on schedule. But I had extra time and sure enough—they said we'd have an hour's delay. No reason was ever given for that delay. Little did we know its significance. Had we left on time we could have landed safely at Las Palmas, before the terrorist bombing.

The seating arrangement that we were about to receive would be for the entire trip to the Canary Islands and return to Los Angeles. As Ted and I reached the head of the line, we were processed by different clerks. Later on, after we left the counter, we compared notes. Ted got seat 28C. I was given 29C. Mine was directly behind his, not alongside like we wanted.

We went back to one of the clerks.

"We were to have seats together. We have business to discuss on the trip," I explained.

"Sorry, sir. The flight is full. A change is impossible," the clerk replied.

His tone was rather firm and so we accepted that seating arrangement grudgingly. It wasn't what we wanted. Have you ever fumed at some inconvenience only to discover later it worked out advantageously? How could I know then that behind this firmness was the Hand of God. Had our seats been changed we both would have perished in the crash.

I was getting into the holiday mood of the other passengers waiting at the airport. There wasn't a soul I knew except Ted, but the festive air of friends and relatives saying good-bye drew me into the group. The delay of our departure went unnoticed in the gaiety of the moment. The cruise of a lifetime was underway . . .

Then a momentary shadow passed me. A number of elderly people, some severely crippled, came into sight. "How can they ever make it?" crossed my mind, and I repeated it to Ted.

"They're from Leisure World," he said. I knew that was a retirement community in Orange County to the south.

There were 41 of their numbers boarding the Pan Am jumbo jet; their average age about 72. They had been booked by a travel agency with the name "Good Time to Travel."

Our flight was called and suddenly the happy hubbub quieted as the words came over the loudspeaker, "Announcing the departure of Pan Am flight number 1736 for New York and Grand Canary Island. Your plane is now loading through gate 17."

I looked at my watch. It was 6:30 P.M. We were on our way.

How did anyone get out?

Photo: Agence Sygma

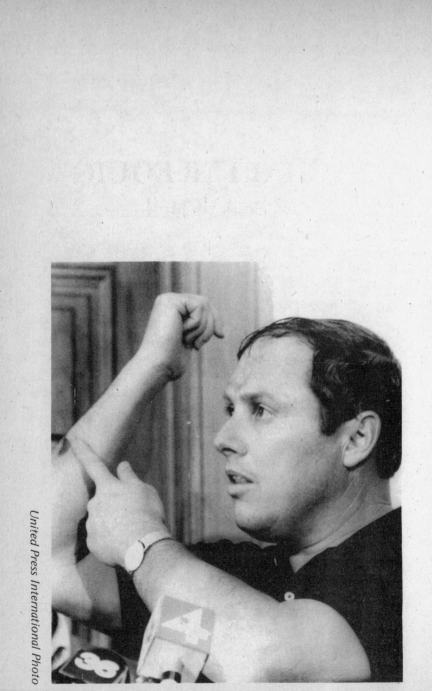

Edward Hess, Phoenix, Arizona,
saved his wife and a trapped woman.

CHAPTER FOUR
Peak of Hell

While our Pan Am charter was winging its way toward New York, still another 747 was being prepared for flight some 5,000 miles away. Royal Dutch Airlines (KLM) flight number 4805 was being fueled and loaded at Schipol Airport in Amsterdam, Holland. She would also head for the Las Palmas airport on Grand Canary Island. It, too, was chartered by a vacation group. So, the KLM jetliner, "the Rhine," would be taking off at about the same time as our Pan Am would be leaving New York for Las Palmas and they too would be landing at Tenerife because of the bomb incident in the Las Palmas flower shop. And we would both be taking off at Tenerife at about the same time.

We had a crew of 14. The same as the Dutch plane. Our passenger total was 368 out of California but we were to pick up 14 more in New York, making 382, a very full airplane. KLM's passengers totaled 234.

Seated next to me on my left were two elderly women, a mother and daughter from Arizona, and seasoned travelers. I was on the aisle directly behind my colleague Ted. The two ladies were between me and the window. The women seemed happy to talk about themselves. The mother, who sat next to the window was 88 years old, I learned. The daughter was 62, and appeared in worse physical condition than her mother.

They chattered about their visits to other countries. It was obvious that they were affluent and well-educated.

"Travel is therapeutic," remarked the daughter to me. "It takes you away from all the tensions in today's environment. I insist that mother takes trips regularly. I can't really afford the time, but she needs me to travel. The travel is good for her."

"Good for me? You know who really needs it," protested the mother. "It does you more good than it does me. That's the reason I'm on this trip, to help you."

They were interesting conversationalists but also heavy drinkers. When the liquor cart came by shortly after takeoff they ordered cocktails. They downed them so fast that they were both ready to reorder before the stewardesses were geared for a second go-around.

They asked me to "flag" a stewardess for them several times. I found myself having to help them get rid of the empties. Stuffing the bottles and glasses in the large pocket in front of my seat. Our seats were in the nonsmoking section so they weren't chainsmokers but they certainly were chain drinkers.

The more they drank, the freer they talked so I eased religion into the conversation. They believed in God—most people do. We discussed the part religion played in each of our lives. They were quick to inform me that they were Presbyterians. They had attended for years and just loved their church and that was that, as they closed the door to any further discussion along this line, and said firmly, "Stewardess: Two more doubles please."

These women were quite badly crippled up, especially the younger one. I found myself catering to their comfort, putting their things under my legs to give them more room, and helping them in and out of their seats. It helped me, too—to pass the time. I found that they were two fascinating people!

The five-hour flight seemed to go fast and soon we were on the approach into Kennedy Airport. Our layover there was supposed to be an hour and a half. Besides taking on fourteen extra passengers, we were getting a brand new crew.

Helping my seat mates into the aisle to deplane actually "married" me to them for the whole stopover. By now it was midnight, Los Angeles time, 3:00 A.M. in New York. I decided to have some coffee.

"Can I bring you both some coffee?" The snack bar was a block away inside the terminal, too far for them to negotiate.

"How kind of you. Yes. Black with sugar."

Ted had left us to make some phone calls to business associates and his family back in California. I drank my coffee and brought two cups to the ladies. Soon Ted returned from his phone calls and pointed out the new passengers that were joining us. Among them was a very large man that I noticed not so much for his size as for his jewelry. Large rings, a large pendant, and more pieces of jewelry here and there. I later found out he was the chef aboard the *M.S. Golden Odyssey* which we were to board.

(I am still unsure whether or not he survived. He did escape from the plane. But later, in the hospital right after the crash, I saw a number of burned and injured people on stretchers. He was one of them. Terribly burned—just terribly burned. His head and face. All over his body. Most of his clothes were gone. But his jewelry was still there. That's how I recognized him.)

More talk and then the stopover was ended by the reboarding announcement.

Waiting for the takeoff I had a chance to chat a moment with the couple behind us. Straight back of me was a single man with an expensive camera slung around his neck. He did not seem to invite conversation. He was quiet but the couple next to him was friendly. They were from Newport Beach.

Being beach people, I told them of my long walks on that beach which I frequently enjoyed in the morning. There were a couple of restaurants that we both enjoyed. Most interesting people.

They were not to survive the crash, but the single man did. And his camera was to be one that captured the most dramatic shots right after the wreck. Can you imagine him bringing his camera out of the inferno with him?

Now that we know not only the degree of terror that awaited, but also a little about me, there are several aspects of these hours before impact which now take on a meaningful dimension.

Take the new crew.

The stewardesses were from several ethnic backgrounds: an exotic girl of Japanese extraction, a beautiful black girl, another who looked Indian. But they were not too friendly; their attitude was colder, contrasting with our previous crew. They seemed solemn, almost to the point of being curt. No outgoingness. They didn't seem very happy. The atmosphere in the plane was changed by it.

I was not the only one to notice this change. Several passengers commented. It was unusual, especially considering it was a chartered flight of vacation-bound passengers. They certainly did not seem to reflect the holiday aspect of our trip. Could their solemnity be some intuitive feeling of what was to come? Only four stewardesses were to survive. So sad. They were so beautiful but so tense.

When you fly eastward at night the dawn explodes quickly. We left New York about 3:00 A.M. We were served one meal. There already came the light of our new day, and the last dawn for most.

The women awoke and admired the sunrise. We were flying high above the clouds, too directly at the rising sun for us to get the full effect of its golden fire. But its glow over the clouds was exquisite. What a show! To this day I can hear their voices praising the colors, the shadows, the golden light.

How much more their words mean in retrospect, that is, putting them in context. I think what she was saying was, "How exquisite is a sunrise when it is the last."

The day had become Sunday, March 27. We were served an airline snack, about an hour out of Las Palmas. It would be about 1:00 in the afternoon when we landed. We were to be taken on a tour of Grand Canary Island, then on to our ship.

But a half hour out of Las Palmas came the captain's announcement about difficulties at Las Palmas and the first news we would be landing at Tenerife instead. "A plane is stalled there with mechanical difficulties," he explained. "It is blocking the runway." Soon he came back on the intercom to report that an explosion had closed Las Palmas airport to all incoming flights.

What about boarding our ship? How would we ever get over to it from Tenerife? were our immediate thoughts.

The terrorist who set that bomb may not have made much of an impact at Las Palmas, but indirectly he killed nearly 600 people at Tenerife. The bomb was hidden inside a vase at the flower shop and it had exploded about noon, injuring eight people, including a saleslady whose wounds were serious.

A telephone call after the explosion, warned that a second bomb had been planted inside the terminal building. It was really the second phone "tip" that prompted the closing of the airport and started a macabre chain of events in the sky. A search failed to uncover any bomb and the airport was reopened later but too late . . . much too late.

"Credit" for the bombing was proudly claimed by the "Movement for Self-Determination and Independence of the Canary Islands." The leader of this group is Antonio Cubillo who fled the islands in the 1960's to set up shop in Algeria. From there his long arm reached out at us.

When Cubillo was informed of the death and terror the bomb caused to hundreds of innocent people at Tenerife he is quoted by the *New York Times* as saying, "We are at war with Spain and these are the consequences. The police ordered the foreign aircrafts diverted to Tenerife which is a suicidal airport. (The crash) . . . was the fault of the control tower. We had nothing to do with it."*

One of the blasphemous slogans of the group is: "Don't trust in God because Franco is in heaven."

The question arises: Was the Hand of God in evidence here? Knowing Cubillo's sarcastic statement about not trusting God, how relevant were these connecting events? We may never know.

And so we finally landed at Tenerife. Its short bumpy runway gave Captain Grubbs and some of us a little thrill on landing we hadn't asked for, but we were in safely. He maneuvered our big airliner up amongst the score of other planes already diverted there and waited . . . and waited. How long our wait would be was a guess. The captain guessed it would be about an hour.

An announcement was made soon after our landing at Tenerife by our tour guide Beau that our cruise ship, the *Golden Odyssey*, might sail the 60 miles from Grand Canary Island to Tenerife Island to pick us up.

Oh, if only it had! One more "if" in the stack.

It takes minutes for a jet to go from Las Palmas to Tenerife but for a ship it's much longer, even for the sleek, modern *Golden Odyssey*. The crew I'm sure measured developments in terms of extra delay. It is hardly ever a gauge of life or death that is applied. For nearly 600 people it would have been life instead of death, had the *Golden Odyssey* come to us. How easy it is to apply that gauge with hindsight.

Geography test:

* *New York Times*, 3/28/77 and 3/29/77.

•   Where and what are the Canary Islands?
•   Are they teeming with birds?

I confess, sitting in Tenerife, wondering for how long, I really didn't care that much. Oh, I had a vague sense of the islands being in the Atlantic off Spain, but that's about all. I wonder how many of the passengers really knew anything much about the Canary Islands? Traveling by jet you can become disoriented and fly right over fascinating places.

Geography lesson:

• The Canary Islands are a group some 70 miles west of Africa. They were given to Spain by a Papal Bull in 1344. They were the last land seen by Christopher Columbus before he crossed the Atlantic.

• There are seven islands in the group: Grand Canary of which the principal city is Las Palmas. Tenerife on which the principal city is Santa Cruz. Their total surface area is a little larger than the state of Delaware.

• The name is derived from the Latin name for the packs of dogs that formerly roamed the islands, called *canae,* not canary birds.

Disoriented? I was.

This did not come to us sitting in the Pan Am 747. About all we could see of even the island of Tenerife were more planes and a big, big mountain.

Had we been flying over Tenerife sightseeing, the Captain could be giving us its vital statistics: 52 miles long, 18 miles wide, shaped like a lamb chop. And ... "The mountain you see is a volcanic peak at the center of the island. It formerly served as a type of beacon for mariners. It is 12,180 feet high. Because natives were convinced the devil lived inside, it is named *Pico de Teide.*"

Enter the devil!

I appreciated the chance to stretch my legs outside the plane. That's when I first saw the "Peak of Hell." Even though I had no knowledge of that mountain, I had a sense of foreboding from it. Even the wind that blew off it brought a sense of foreboding. It was a strong whimsical wind. I felt it blew hard from the Peak of Hell itself.

At the top of the mountain were thick clouds. Each time I looked they seemed to be lower. When you are waiting, waiting, waiting for a moment of departure that might come at any moment, whatever you see you evaluate as a threat to that departure. As a possible cause of still more delay. That's what the cloud spelled to me. And unfortunately my spelling was correct. Within the hour we were enveloped in that cloud.

It was a foreboding shroud from the foreboding mountain borne to us by a foreboding wind.

Color it grey—dark grey.

It greyed my spirits, as it must have threatened the spirits of the Pan Am crew and also the KLM captain. Being shunted into Tenerife was bad enough but to be trapped here by that cloud was unthinkable. Apparently, the Dutch captain was anxious to cut down the effect of this delay. He decided to refuel here, using this time instead of at Las Palmas later.

One can only stand in awe at the sequence of events.

Do you remember the nursery rhyme about the house that Jack built? "This is the straw that went into the brick that went into the wall of the house that Jack built." Or something to that effect.

Well, this was the delay, and this was the wind, and this was the mountain, and this was the fog from the mountain— all materials that built the catastrophe. In this instance we aren't yet sure just who "Jack" was. But it certainly wasn't God. All the delays and decisions were strictly manmade. God entered the scene after man and the elements messed things up. He came with deliverance in His hands.

Our Captain sounded really annoyed at the KLM plane when he announced to us that there was not enough room for us to taxi around it. We would have to wait another

[handwritten marginalia:] No! God orchestrated all of mans doings. Scripture is very plain, stating repeatedly "God causes the disasters"

half hour until the KLM captain had completed taking on his load of jet fuel.

Somehow time begins to recede into distance when you are flight weary. What's another half hour? Disappointing, but not intolerable, and not as intolerable as that first hour of delay. We were becoming veterans of delay. Another half hour we could take in stride.

Waiting. Waiting. My thoughts were champing now. That 747 could have flown the entire voyage of the *Golden Odyssey* in the time we were waiting.

I got up again and stood by my partner Ted who was now stretching his legs in the aisle.

"How old do you think that fellow is?" Ted nodded down the aisle.

"In his 80s," I guessed.

"And maybe 90," Ted said.

"In all my travels," Ted continued, "I have never seen a group quite like this. So many old people. You can't blame Leisure World. Only about 41 came from there. Many of these look like they have graduated Leisure World."

I chuckled. But it did give you a weird feeling.

One woman was in a body cast. Another had her arm in a cast raised awkwardly. A man was walking up and down the aisle with a cane, half dragging his poor old body, evidently the victim of a stroke.

"Ted," I asked, "What are we doing here? What kind of a thing have you gotten us into?"

He laughed.

"You know what it reminds me of?" I asked. "It reminds me of a movie I saw on TV not so long ago called *The Ship of Fools.*"

I reminded Ted that it was a movie about a cruise ship. The people who were taking that cruise were dead, but did not know it.

"The people on *The Ship of Fools* were sailing into eternity. Some of our passengers remind me of them."

These were the final words I ever spoke to Ted. Words about eternity. The "Fasten Your Seat Belts" sign flashed on. Our own ship to "eternity" was about to sail.

It was to prove totally a trip to eternity for the KLM. One lady left the KLM plane at Tenerife and didn't get back in time. This reduced the passenger complement to a total of 248. It would be interesting to know who that lady was and why she did not reboard. The Hand of God, no doubt.

All of the passengers that boarded KLM Flight 4805 at Schipol Airport in Amsterdam were Easter vacationers bound for various resort hotels in the Grand Canary Islands. It was cold and rainy in Holland that morning with some fog and spitting snow.

If the Pan Am passengers were mainly old, then the KLM passengers were mainly young. There were 48 children, including three infants. Their parents were in their 30s and 40s. All except 10 of the passengers were from the Netherlands. Four were from Germany. Two from Australia and four from the United States. The four Americans were traveling together. They were Mr. D.R.E. Gilles, 49, and his wife, Jane, 48; Mrs. T. Twist, 21, and her 21-month-old infant Melissa. All were formerly of Rochester, N.Y. but were then living in Venray, Netherlands. Mr. Gilles and Mrs. Twist both worked for the Rand Xerox Company in Venray.

The brilliant captain of the KLM 747 was Jacob Veldhuyzen van Zanten. He was 51, five years younger than our captain. He lived in Amsterdam. He had 25 years of experience and was cover pilot in KLM's in-flight magazine. His face was also featured in their dependable, on time Dutch ads.

I saw the tail of van Zanten's KLM go by our window. Now we were moving too.

Surrounded by old and crippled souls, encapsulated in the 747 fuselage, enshrouded in fog and stalked by the Peak of Hell, I began to yearn for some of the pleasures I had paid some 2,000 dollars for: the ship's bunk, the food, the service, the sunlight, the sights, the new horizons.

The slow taxiing of the plane was welcome movement compared to four static hours, but a snail's pace compared to the volition of my body and soul.

The oriental stewardess walked by silently and expressionless, looking left and right to see if all seat belts were fastened. Her name was Sachiko Hirano, from New York City, faithfully performing in the last 10 minutes of her life.

So were stewardesses Mari Asar also of New York; Marilyn Luker of Philadelphia; Aysel Sharp of Arlington, Virginia; Christine Ekelund, Carol Thomas, Miguel Torrech and Luisa Flood, all of New York City. Sheer courage from each.

One purser was to die—Francoise De Beaulieu also of New York—while the other—Dorothy Kelly of New Hampshire—was to miraculously live through it all. Surviving stewardesses were Susanne Donovan of Harrisburg, Pennsylvania; Joan Jackson of Nashville, Tennessee; and Carla Johnson of New York. Good people!

Remarkably the cockpit crew were all going to survive: Flight Engineer George Warns of Blairstown, New Jersey; Copilot Robert Bragg of Howard Beach, Long Island, New York; and Captain Victor Grubbs of Centerport, Long Island, New York.

on p. 16 it stated only 6mph

Finally the stewardesses cleared the aisles, having buckled up ready for takeoff. We were rapidly taxiing down the main runway, with Captain Grubbs peering through the fog looking for a third exit off the runway to permit the other plane to takeoff. KLM was already in place for takeoff down the same runway.

How silent now were the 382 passengers. Like in a theatre with the curtain about to rise. Even the four engines seemed barely to whisper as Captain Grubbs moved his 231-foot craft along the runway, cautiously, smoothly.

It was a full plane! The basic accommodations of a 747 call for 48 first class passengers and 337 economy class passengers: a grand total of 385. Empty, the same plane weighs 180 tons; but full load, could takeoff with 200 tons more of passengers' baggage, and fuel. A truly great airplane. A veritable Leviathan of the air, but as we were to find out in a few moments—a delicate, fragile bird on the ground.

Captain Grubbs had passed a third exit ramp. Grubbs counted it number two as not only was the first ramp clogged with planes but this third one was narrow and severely angled back. Obviously not usable—not the one. He knew the tower hadn't cleared KLM for takeoff. Now the tower was waiting for Grubbs to report we had turned off on some exit ramp and were clear of the runway.

But what about Captain van Zanten in the KLM unexplainably making his moves? He somehow thought we were clear of the runway. How could he "know" this? Nobody said we were. Who or what authorized him to start his takeoff roll? Had he mentally calculated that the Pan Am, taxiing at normal speed, had enough time to reach its exit ramp? Had he included in these mental calculations not only a 20 miles per hour taxiing speed but exit three, rather than exit four?

Had he heard only the last three words of Captain Grubbs reply, *"We'll report when clear of runway"*? A possibility—there was radio static.

Had the frustrating delay and some Amsterdam delights tampered with his judgment and timing? Had he seen a momentary blowing away of the ground fog and decided to get out before Tenerife closed because of marginal visibility?

Van Zanten gunned his fuel-laden jet!

Captain Grubbs and Copilot Bragg saw lights on the runway ahead. Blurred by the ever-moving fog their depth perception was playing tricks. The lights almost looked stationary, especially considering that they were supposed to be stationary. But they were growing unmistakably larger . . .

That was when he shouted at the Tower into his mike, "We are still on the runway!"

Captain Grubbs watched in unbelief at the approaching lights, "He'll kill us all!"

"Get off! Get off!" Bragg yelled at our Captain.

Grubbs gunned his engine and turned hard left in a frantic attempt to get off the runway and out of the KLM's path.

That moment was when I felt the wheels slump downward, followed in a second by the impact.

That was when there was instant fire.

Falling ceiling.

Explosion.

Screams.

Curses, moans.

Havoc.

Silence.

Do you have a vague feeling you have been here before? Well, that is what I felt, like I had lived this moment before.

The psychologists have a name for this phenomenon— déjà vue. It means "already seen." They recognize it, but cannot explain it. Some psychologists think it happens as a result of having had a dream which was never fully remembered. Dreams are sometimes prophetic. When the dreamed of events arrives, the person then has that sense of familiarity.

Maybe. But could the Hand of God have something to do with this strange familiarity? Was I closer to God at this moment and therefore closer to timelessness? An instant supply of calm, lucidity and superhuman strength?

I was standing. Searing flames had enveloped me. Crackling, smoking, chaos. My two seatmates had disappeared into the floor. (Looking back now I wonder just what caused this.) The older lady at the window went down first, the daughter followed. Our roof was sliced by the KLM's landing gear. Explosions and wrenching stresses were twisting and rearranging our plane.

Another explosion blasted searing fragments into me. It blasted between me and Ted and he was gone. As close as those seats were that's how close. Inches were miles all over the plane. After that I never saw Ted. The forces and their speed are indescribable. People inches apart were separated. One-to-life, one-to-death.

I was back at home holding the Bible with my mother. Don't ask me how. I saw the tears in her eyes as she prayed for my safe return.

At that moment I cried out: "In the name of Jesus, through Your shed blood, I stand upon Your Word."

I began to move. I was moving through the heaving, exploding havoc.

"I stand upon Your Word . . . Stand upon Your Word . . . Stand upon Your Word! . . ."

I was being moved—propelled?—pushed? Where did the strength come from? The direction? The desire?

I wasn't out yet. Would I ever be?

Happy reunion. Richard Sinnett (rear bandaged hand)
and his wife Kay (r) hug greeters.

All that remained of two proud birds.

United Press International Photo

CHAPTER FIVE
Shadrach's Furnace

"I stand upon Your Word! I stand upon Your Word!"
I have had some marvelous spiritual experiences throughout my life. But I have never sensed the presence of the Holy Spirit as I did in that indescribable fury.

The Spirit of God was so strong. It was as if a blanket of peace was thrown over me—I wasn't numb—a lucid calm enveloped me. I was in the midst of a fiery bomb yet I knew all was well. I did not move in panic. I did not move in fear. I did not even move as if my life depended on it. That wasn't me—no one can act that way. I knew it was beyond man—any man.

You might say I did not move at all. But that I was moved. The Spirit of God moving me, directing me.

My head ducked a piece of white hot debris hurtling at 100 miles an hour. Enough to decapitate me. Somehow my head darted just in time as it whistled past.

Again I shouted, "I stand upon Your Word! I stand upon Your Word!" Each time I proclaimed those words new hope and new strength surged in me. Here in the midst of the worst human tragedy I could imagine was the greatest spiritual experience I could dream of.

What does one do trapped in a cauldron of death? Get out the 747 brochure and check out the exits? Listen to the moans of anguish? Call information? You are so alone.

How about help from a stewardess? The purser? The captain himself? They're all busy living or dying. You have to go higher. The President of the United States? Higher, still.

In the moment of reckoning, you do have a friend in a high place. Just one. He is never too busy or out to lunch. He will make house calls, anywhere . . . He came to me.

Another object hurtled at me. It was a huge piece of debris. It would impale me. It was white hot. It was massive. The speed made it impossible to avoid. But that moment the anointing of the Holy Spirit was so heavily upon me I was literally imbued with "power from on high." My arms shot up. As large as it was, and as fast as it was hurtling through the air, it was deflected. I was Superman! I turned around, facing the back. What I saw I shall never forget. Faces. Bleeding faces. Burning faces. Anguished faces. Stony faces. They were milling about. Some cursed. Some bravely yielded to death. Some collapsed and others stepped all over them.

I moved. If you don't move, you cost lives, your life, the lives of others.

There is not time to ponder. I was programmed to survive. You do what has to be done. I was no part of the cacophony of sound. I was not part of the melee of destruction. I was not part of the gripping fear.

I seemed separated from all of this and I knew that my insulation from death was due to my prayers. I said it again, "I stand upon Your Word. I stand upon Your Word." New strength.

That hurtling metal had driven me back so I could see a light splotch through the smoke. A gash in the cabin ceiling. The sky was visible through it. Part of the roof had been blown off. There was my escape hatch but it was so high. Have you ever noted the ceiling height in a jumbo jet?

How I ever lifted myself up to that height, I will never know. Did I climb up the back of the seats? Did I step on that piece of debris that I deflected? How was my bone-tired six-foot, 250-pound frame lifted some 10 feet to grab the ragged edges of that blasted fuselage? And once my hands were on that knife edge, how could a non-athletic heavyweight hoist himself up and then out? I was somehow able to hurtle my body up and over the edge of that opening. There was no place to put my legs to help me do this. Although my hands were cut by that ragged metal as they pulled my weight up, there wasn't a cut or bruise on my torso. Measured in terms of my own strength, it was impossible!

How it happened, I may never know. But happen it did. I was able to lift myself up, fly out through that hole in the cabin roof and then throw myself over the side onto the wing.

There was slippery oil on the wing but I knew I must keep moving and get off that fuel-filled wing quickly. I had to get away from this fire-wracked aircraft. I knew it had another explosion in the making. How could I do it from this height?

Some people had already jumped from the wing. They had fatally injured some below in that manner. Under ordinary conditions, the 30-foot jump would give you a reason to pause. But it did not concern me in the least. There was no choice. I slid further out on the wing still higher and hurtled myself out into the air.

I was again "standing on the Word" as I jumped. I hit the ground, standing on my feet. The instant I hit the ground it turned to praise.

As I hobbled away from the burning plane, my praise of the Lord was unabashed. It poured forth from me not only in English but in other tongues. I shouted the glory of God in languages I had never learned!

I now wondered what might have happened to Mr. and Mrs. Mario Tyzbir who were the last people who had any remote chance of getting out on the runway side of the plane. I was to hear Mario's story on our return flight to Los Angeles from Tenerife, but I'll let him tell it later on . . .

I finally reached a safe distance from the plane, perhaps

100 yards. I turned around and looked back. I expected to see Ted following behind, because he was a younger and more athletic man. He wasn't anywhere in sight. In fact, I was quite alone at that moment.

I was not the only one whose escape was by the mercy of God.

Back in row 34 were our friends, the Hecks. Floy sat hypnotized by the flames and watching as her Leisure World traveling companions succumbed. Then she heard her husband Paul commanding her, "Floy, get up!" He led her out on to the wing. When she hurtled to the ground, she injured her leg and couldn't rise. She just lay there asking Jesus to help her. He did. Soon she could crawl from the burning wreckage to safety. Paul Heck survived, too, but she didn't see him again until two days later in a United States hospital.

The Mario Tyzbirs lived in Leisure World. He had done well in the machine tool business for 30 years. "Ham" Tyzbir back in seat 26A said, "My wife Irene and I tried for two years to get on this cruise but it was always filled to capacity.

"When the crash came it sounded like everything was crumbling. Instantly there was fire. When that happened the old man next to me just passed out. A heart attack, I suppose. I unbuckled my seatbelt, got my wife unbuckled, and we crawled over the man. Finally I was in the aisle and if I had reached out I could touch the fire. There were only three of us who escaped through the roof. Norman Williams was one of them.

"I saw Norman as I turned in the aisle. He was going through a jagged hole in the ceiling of the plane. He was in seat 29. From 28 to 31 the KLM landing gear gouged a hole on the left side of the plane. So, following Norman saved my life.

"After one explosion I crawled up on top of the chairs—we were the only two left. The people all around us were utterly immobile. I pulled myself up on a steel girder. Then lying on my stomach I reached down and grabbed my wife's hand. At that instant a second explosion occurred. The concussion blew her clear back into the plane. It blew me clear out on the wing, which was slippery with fuel oil, and I went off it toward the ground. I thought I was safe but people were yelling and screaming at me to 'get away from the plane! Get away from the plane, it's going to explode!'

"What really got me was the third explosion. I wasn't quite over to the grass yet. I went into shock. I had been cool until the third explosion but when I saw that, I started to shake. I never shook in the plane. I looked back. What I saw made me thank God. Oh, how I thank God I made it out! But my dear wife didn't. It really was like getting out of a furnace."

Another told how her escape was also miraculous. She felt Someone was watching over her. A guardian angel. Who could doubt it?

Edward Hess yelled at his wife Mary to follow him as he led to the rear where the plane had split apart. He lost her in the black smoke—an explosion blew away the smoke. He reached over a pile of burning rubble, grabbed her and managed to pull her almost over the debris. But he could not hang on and she fell back into the flames burning her legs. He grabbed down for her again—this time she followed.

She said, "Somebody gave me a push from the rear." Yet nobody followed her out. She was the last to escape the dying jumbo jet.

Who could have pushed her out from inside that fiery furnace? Could it have been that same Person seen by King Nebuchadnezzar standing with Shadrach, Meshach and Abednego inside the furnace heated up to seven times its normal temperature? The Son of God?

That Hand had saved many but survival for all wasn't possible that day.

Blood-curdling screams of people being burned alive

were mixed with the cries of people calling for loved ones, moans, curses, and other indescribable sounds of human agony and rage.

Ragged pieces of shrapnel-like metal exploded into people's faces and bodies in warlike ways.

Edgar Ridout, 33, a businessman from San Diego, tried to pull an elderly lady from the seat. He did not know she had been sliced in two. Only the top half of her came out.

A brave stewardess inflated a life raft so that her people could safely jump from the plane onto something soft. There was an explosion. The pretty stewardess was decapitated.

Screaming people trampled on an old lady fallen in the aisle. Who knows whether she was dead or dying? Others sat quietly in their seats as if transfixed, their own clothes on fire. Like burning wax mannequins.

As I look back at it, I know that through my having trusted on the Word of Jesus, He had confirmed that I was an heir, a joint heir, of His love. I had learned that His Word is good in any crisis. New meaning to His promise, "All things are possible to them that believe."

By now I was out of that hell. I spotted a crew member kneeling on the grass between me and the plane. He was beating the ground. It was Captain Grubbs.

When the impact came a huge piece of fuselage was ripped off the top of the Pan Am plane. When Copilot Bragg reached for the fire handles above his head, they were gone. Immediately the cockpit floor gave way. Grubbs and Bragg were dropped into the first class cabin below. He couldn't switch off his engines. The flight deck disintegrated.

Somehow Captain Grubbs found himself thrown out on the wing. He slid off to the ground. His was the agony of self-blame and he beat the ground. Dorothy Kelly, purser in that first class section, followed the same escape route. She saw him kneeling, rocking back and forth, and mumbling, "What have I done to these people?" Dorothy made him get up and move to safety.

"It was so heavenly to sink down in the cool green grass wet with rain," Grubbs recalled later. Although overcome with remorse over the tragedy, he knew in his heart that it wasn't his fault. He was to survive his second- and third-degree burns.

My own hands were bleeding. They'd been cut open by the weight of my body pulling them against the razor-like edges of the fuselage roof. My clothing was splattered with blood. A jagged hole was cut in the knee of my trousers where I had managed to lift it up and hurl my body out. My left foot throbbed with pain.

A distant explosion sent clouds of smoke and flame skyward behind our burning Pan Am plane. Remembering the traffic jam of planes at the terminal, and still not knowing that we had been struck by the KLM plane, I thought our accident had touched off another fire.

Just then, as I watched, a massive explosion rent the Pan Am plane. The entire wreckage blew up in flames. I recoiled at the sight.

I turned to hobble away. Praise for my deliverance was still filling my heart. First in English, "Praised be the Lord. Praised be the Lord." Then English seemed inadequate to express my gratitude—I broke out again praying with the Spirit.

A score of people were moving across the grass ahead of me. A score more were behind me. Some were being helped by another as badly burned as they. One man asked a passerby for help: "Sorry," was the reply, and he lifted up his hands, fingers blown off at the knuckles.

My foot was broken but I didn't know it yet. I continued to limp away. Joy eclipsed all pain.

Deliverance from that hellstorm, torture and destruction. I was joyous that my devotion to God through the years had, in effect, created a crisis "hot line" to Him. He had responded.

Even if I had been required to die in that fiery furnace, I

know that I would have gone into death and to meet my Maker without fear and with the same joyous feelings.

I remembered as I praised the Lord, "When thou walkest through the fire thou shalt not be burned. Neither shall the flame kindle upon thee."

I had no burns. Not a hair had been singed.

It was now probably 5:10 or 5:11. A few were still jumping from the flames.

One frantic husband raced back toward the fiery wreckage, "My wife, I must get to her. I thought she was with me." The burnt passenger was restrained by Captain Grubbs.

One survivor was taking pictures. It was the man who sat behind me with the expensive camera around his neck. I found out later he was David Wiley, 29, an electronics technician of Palo Alto. His only injury was a gash on the back of his head. His camera escaped without harm.

No more people emerged. There was only the whimper of the wounded and dying—the roar of the flames.

Edward Hess, 39, a former Navy air traffic controller, was one of the last out. He suffered only minor injuries, but his wife, Mary, suffered burns over 50 percent of her body. According to Hess, suffocation became an additional threat as hot, acrid, black smoke choked out all oxygen.

There were scores of acts of bravery. Most will go unsung, curtained by the flames and smoke. Some failed, others were successful. The heroes of failure just as valiant as the heroes of escape. God's knowledge is never obscured by anything.

Still another was successful. He helped save two others in his family. Leading them through the flames toward a hole he could vaguely see in the plane's side. In the nick of time they hurtled twenty feet to the ground just before an explosion which caused the nose of the plane to drop. This hero grabbed an arm of one before he jumped. She was on fire. Taking an arm he pulled her across the field and rolled out the fire.

Rescuers were now arriving in great numbers. They carried the injured and the burnt and helped the crippled. Some drove cars right on to the field and up to the crash scene. Others came from nearby homes with waterjugs and towels to help the survivors. Tenerife is filled with brave men. Many were injured. Some stormed the exploding wreckage itself to snatch the living right out of the arms of death.

I watched the burnt being helped. I motioned away those concerned by the blood splattered on my clothes and running from my head, and pointed to others in far more need.

These outside sights are somehow more vivid to me than the holocaust itself. Inside, it all happened so fast. It transcended the ability of human senses to cope with it. All circuits of the brain were overloaded. When you are inside an explosion, it is indescribable—unrecordable by the mind.

Outside the plane, an explosion can be placed in its proper frame of reference. "There goes explosion number four at the tail."

But to be inside an explosion . . . !

I can still see the engines whirling and the jetting fumes, sparks flying. The engines were on fire but still roaring on. No wonder Mr. Heck stayed clear of them.

I can also still see the KLM explosion and flames. You need distance to gain perspective. It gives you sensory perspective. Time gives you philosophical and spiritual perspective. I did not have that kind of perspective as the evacuation of survivors began. I have a little now, and will talk about this later.

I wrapped a handkerchief around the flooding from cuts on my hand. My gratitude at surviving would not have been dimmed if I had lost a hand. How much better off was I than those back inside and the burnt all around me . . . I was actually standing and breathing.

Now it was dusk. The fog and wind was there. So was

Pico de Teide but I was still there. I could look up at it and laugh.

Now I was standing alone about 50 feet from Captain Grubbs, who a few moments before was beating the ground with both fists. He and Copilot Bragg stood watching the final disintegration of their plane. Although no longer beating the ground, the captain's body language spoke of inner torment—"What have I done—" albeit knowing in his heart it was not his fault.

Copilot Bragg was standing beside Captain Grubbs, still not aware his own leg was broken. And I was standing on a foot I didn't know was broken. We learned there are greater anguishes . . .

The villagers were carrying some, tenderly walking others to taxis, cars, and ambulances.

After the more desperately injured had been rushed from the field, it came my turn. I was driven to a small building near the terminal, a sort of waiting room. It was now being used as an assembly point. There was less than 60 in that room.

The badly injured were placed on the floor. We who could sit up, used the benches. We tried to comfort one another. Such a bond is forged in tragedy. It's a leveler in humanity. Oh, that we could be so kind in all phases of life!

A terribly burnt woman was carried in on a stretcher and placed on the bench next to me. She was in such agony. She kept crying for her husband. There was no way I or anyone else there could help her.

"Oh, my God, where's my husband? Oh, my God! Oh, my God!"

Beside me now was a Japanese man who, I remembered, had been sitting with his wife across from me in the center portion of the plane. She was so gracious the way she helped others with their coats and belongings.

"I'm glad to see you," I said to him. "Your wife?"

He shook his head slowly, "I had a hold of her. But I lost her in the fire."

I bowed my head and broke at his loss. A woman came over and put her arm around me. "Be thankful you're alive," she said comfortingly. Apparently she thought I lost a loved one.

I told her, "I was with my business associate, a younger man, but I don't see him. I don't think he made it. I hope I'm wrong."

"My husband is gone," she said quietly.

And here she was consoling me and others too. Such beauty of character.

Sensing my grief for her, she explained, "My husband and I have enjoyed such wonderful trips together. We have been so privileged. We mutually decided that should an air tragedy ever strike and take one of us, that the grief of it should not ruin the rest of his or her life."

I marveled at her strength to be able to implement the philosophy with such immediacy. Without tears she was able to recall their agreement.

"Does your arm pain you?"

"Would you like more space to stretch out?"

"How fortunate we are."

People, themselves in shock, helping other people in whatever small way they could.

The villagers helping too; they came from their little houses all around the airport with bottles of water, pieces of clothing and love.

One survivor walked around near-naked in shock, most of the clothes burned off of him. Pneumonia is a real risk under such conditions. I motioned a local man with some clothing over his arm. He covered him up ever so gently.

Another came along with a bucket of something that looked like axle grease. It was to help stop bleeding. My right hand was still bleeding profusely, my left hand not so badly. He scooped some grease up and smeared it all over my hands. It worked.

One by one they were now taking us out of that room and dispatching us to nearby hospitals and clinics in Santa

Cruz. It is hard to judge time but it must have been almost an hour when they got to me. I was about the last. Two women helped me into a car. I apologized for getting blood all over their clothing.

"Da Nada. Da Nada," they kept saying. Meaning it is nothing.

"Gracias a Dios," I kept repeating, a basic course in Spanish which I had taken in recent years was coming in handy. "Thanks to God."

They both nodded in agreement.

A man was driving the car. It was not a taxi, but his own private car. I was getting blood all over the upholstery. I was concerned and apologized to him. Again, "Da Nada. Da Nada." He was a young man in his 20s. He spoke a little English and wanted to know if I spoke Dutch, which I didn't. "I go Germany today, but then I not go. I now know why not go." The Hand again.

It was just 15 minues to the hospital, about eight miles. I was moving further away from the scene of the disaster, better able to look back and start to sort it out a little. Separated for the first time from suffering survivors I was feeling the reality even more. It wasn't a dream, it had really happened.

I had clearness of mind. I was shattered by what I had seen in the past hour, but I was not in shock. It had been a horrible thing to be in the midst of and to see, hear and feel. But no "shakes." I was still calm and in fairly good control. Still, I was different, changed. No longer the tourist who arrived that afternoon in Tenerife. A tourist sees from the outside. I was to be forever a part of Tenerife and Tenerife a part of me. And that flow of life through me was being expressed in feeling *a feeling of God's presence,* a feeling of "Gracias a Dios."

It was still foggy. The windshield wiper was on the blink. He had to reach out and move it by hand from time to time. Sunday night and people filled narrow streets and sidewalks of Santa Cruz. Nothing changes. He sat on the horn and kept moving.

It was a hospital we pulled up to. I had on my coat with my passport and other important papers, including my traveler's checks. I had kept my coat on because it was to be such a short flight from Tenerife to Las Palmas. How glad I was for this little blessing. I kept my valuables in and the fire out. (Think I'll keep you, old raggedy friend.)

When I got out of the car I offered the man some money. He shook his head emphatically. Nobody at Tenerife—*I mean nobody*—local residents, taxi drivers, nurses, doctors, accepted a dime or any gift from survivors. They gave whatever they had to give.

I don't recall the name of the hospital. "Residencia" something. Six or seven stories. I waited quite a while in the admittance area. By now my left foot was impossible to stand on. I could only hop. Several people helped me into a wheelchair. They were busy with desperately urgent cases. I didn't mind waiting. No burns. Not a hair on my head . . .

When they finally got around to me, they really moved fast. They practically ran me through the hallways, and the kitchen area. All the people in white aprons jumped to the side as we went sailing through. Not killed in the crash, not killed by taxi, how embarrassing to die in a wheelchair accident!

Into the elevator and up several floors, along the hallway, finally entering this private room. Small, clean, plain. No, the word is *stark*.

They lifted me out of the wheelchair and laid me down on this white sheeted bed. And they left.

It was so clean, so white, so quiet. Blessed quiet, blessed bed.

I just lay there with my clothes on, surrounded by those clean sheets, clean white blankets, clean white pillow, clean white ceiling, clean white curtains, and clean white walls.

Slowly a red stain began to color the sheets as blood continued to drip from my hands. It was the only color in that white room.

My eyes were on an object attached to the wall opposite me. It was a crucifix.

As a Protestant, the cross without Christ is what I look up to. We worship a resurrected Christ, we have a thing about that. Not a crucified Christ. Yet, as I lay in the white room here and now, so aware of my own be-ing, I became aware of His own suffering. I realized ever so keenly that everything He did was for me. Suddenly His suffering meant more to me. His hours of bleeding and hurting on that cross became personal. Both the empty and the full cross meant more.

I had these clean white sheets and a beating heart instead of lying out in those ashes—just because of Him.

The crucifix became a precious thing to me, leading me again into a reinforcement of the gratitude that had sprung from my lips out on that runway. I lay there gazing at it. Later, whenever anybody came into the room I would point to it and say, "Gracias a Dios." They would cross themselves. It didn't bother me anymore. Another hangup had burned in the crash.

One extreme to the other. From pandemonium to peace.

The protection of the Lord was even sweeter than the protection of the clean white walls and the clean white sheets. And the crucifix reminded me.

More than relieved I was here, that I was alive. Sounds from the hallway. The sound of people was reassuring music at that time. Some of it was heavy though.

"My God! My God!" came agonized screams. The torment of excruciating pain from widespread burns, broken bones, and open wounds reminded me that all was not clean and white and peaceful outside my room. Some pains cannot be relieved.

Several more hours before I was treated. A team of

doctors, nurses, and trainees came in en masse. My foot was bandaged as were my two hands. There was no time to check for broken bones or even for a wash. They had so much to do for so many.

As fast as the team burst into the room, they burst out again. And I was alone again.

I began to think about my mother. I prayed that God would protect her when she heard the news. I prayed that she would not be alone when she heard it. I realized that it was midday in California, Sunday, and that it was not likely that she would have the television set on. That's good.

I had no idea of the exact time. I had lost the watch off my wrist during the explosions. I had not slept in a day and a half, but I was still wide awake.

I just lay there, grateful.

Occasionally, a doctor or a nurse would look in as the night hours went by. They too, were grateful. They expressed it by their faces, the words they spoke and the hand on my forehead or the pat on my cheek. It was human warmth they expressed—openly, genuinely. God has built such wonderful people. They're hidden throughout the world for such a time as this.

It was in the early morning hours that the "team" returned. Finally they took off my dirty and torn clothes. They bathed me and gave me a pair of hospital pajamas, four sizes too small!

They extracted pieces of metal from my hair and scalp. They dug for tiny fragments of metal under my skin. It had been liquid when it hit me, then it solidified. These pellets kept coming out of me for days, spotting the bedsheets with skinny beebees when I awoke.

Now, the "team" dressed me in clean bandages, and looked me over for other injuries. Then they left.

Alone again in the clean white room, I did not sleep. I gazed at the crucifix and remembered His suffering. For me!

The debris of destiny — 583 dead.

Photo: Henri Bureau/Sygma

CHAPTER SIX
People Help People

It was 3 P.M. on Sunday, March 27. Back in California my sister's phone rang.

"Is this Mrs. Olsen?" a lady's voice asked.

"Yes."

"Mrs. Virginia Olsen?"

"Yes, this is she."

"This is Laurie, Lynne Younes' sister."

"Oh, yes," replied my sister, recalling that Lynne Younes was my business colleague's wife, but not suspecting what she was about to hear next.

"Lynne asked me to call you. The flight that Norman and Ted were on has crashed in the Canary Islands."

There was long silence, and then her voice sounding shocked and stunned, "Are . . . are you sure?"

"It has been confirmed that it was their flight."

Another silence.

Virginia's mouth opened but she could not speak. As tears poured forth, she motioned her husband to take the phone. While he proceeded to get all the information that Laurie had, Virginia turned on the all-news radio station. Sure enough, they were reporting details of a crash.

Virginia listened in total shock. She wanted to pray but the words were not there. She was too stunned. There was only disbelief. Could it be some mix-up?

"Jesus, Jesus," she buried her face in her hands. "Oh, dear God." Over and over she sobbed these words as her husband completed his conversation and then phoned Lynne Younes.

Lynne said she was on her way to Los Angeles airport to get survivor information from Pan American Airlines. She would keep in touch.

No sooner had he hung up the phone, when it rang again. It was my mother. She was returning a call Virginia had made earlier to her. Now it was Virginia's turn to call time out.

"Mother, can I get back to you?"

Virginia went over to the fireplace. She was joined by Jerry.

"You do it—my voice . . . I just can't."

Her husband led in prayer as they all held hands in a circle. At the close, Jerry exclaimed, "He's alive, I just know it and feel it!"

Now it was time to tell Mother of the crash. At first Virginia decided to have her daughter call and say they would be over in the evening. But that would arouse suspicion. She would just drive over and do it.

On the way they kept the car radio tuned to KFWB. No good news, two planes—747's—had crashed, 500 had perished but there were some survivors. They turned it off after awhile. It was too hard.

Jerry kept reassuring Virginia that I might be among the survivors. Virginia "read" his words as just that—reassurance. They had to be realistic.

As they approached the house, they turned the radio on again. Now they heard there were maybe 30 survivors. Well, there was a small chance—just enough to let hope back in.

As they drove up to the front of the house, the report came over the radio that the confirmed number of survivors was 58. Almost twice the number reported.

When Mother met them at the door, their hope was on the upbeat.

"What a surprise! Come in. How nice of you to drive over. I hope you can spend the evening."

Mother did not know. They could see it. They would tell her.

"What brings you here?" Mother asked.

"News that is not too good," replied Virginia.

"Is it something to do with Norman?"

"Yes. It is."

Mother is a strong woman. She did not cry, but Virginia could see the trepidation in her face, when she blurted out the shocking facts.

Jerry went over and turned on the radio and they all listened as the reports rolled in.

Virginia was concerned for Mother. Mother's face and ears were red. Was there the possibility of her having a stroke? But Mother reached for the Bible. "We are going to call on God to spare Norman," she said.

All three put their hands on the Bible as Mother led in prayer. In strong words she let God know her petition, reminding Him of their prayers before I left.

Then they waited together. Not knowing made it a contest between faith and fear. One minute the one, the next minute the other. Virginia was reminded of the time her son passed away eight years ago with leukemia. Even though that had been a shock, it had come at least somewhat expected.

This crash came totally unexpected, undreamed of, unthinkable. The airlines had built up such a remarkable safety record—safer than driving yourself to the store.

California being the point of origin of the Pan Am plane, KFWB was doing in-depth coverage of the tragedy. Now the total number of survivors was being reported as 78. I could be one of them, they told each other.

Phone calls began coming in from people who knew that Ted and I were on the plane.

"We now have a list of survivors," said the radio announcer, and he began to read the names on that list.

Mother again reached for the Bible and all three began to pray fervently now. "Please, God, let Norman's name be read."

The list was in alphabetical order. Name after name was read. The very last name—*Norman Williams!*

The living room of that house became wild. Shouting, crying and laughing. Norman was alive!

"I knew something was wrong when you arrived," Mother now told Virginia. "I could see it in your face—the concern."

It was 5 P.M. They decided to drive back to their house, bringing Mother along to stay with them so she would not be alone.

On the way to the Olsen house, with the car radio on, the list of survivors was read several times, again repeating "Norman Williams." But still the question mark, "How badly hurt is Norman?" So many were badly burned—had already died from injuries.

The news was left on during dinner. There was no thought of going to sleep.

At about 11 P.M. the phone rang.

"It's the Canary Islands," shouted Virginia.

The operator put me on.

"I'm fine, just minor injuries," I assured them. "How's Mother?"

I had to keep the conversation brief because others were waiting to call relatives.

Back in my white room, I heard the winds of the previous day picking up again, terrible winds from off that peak. I still could not erase the events from my mind. Pictures would return. Big pictures—the white hot object hurtling at me. I really must have been Superman to deflect it. But I knew it was Super God. Little pictures—an old couple in the middle of the plane. She was combing his long white hair. Such beautiful white hair for a man. Every time he leaned forward, she would re-comb his hair.

I asked that the door of my room be left open so I could see the activities in the hall. Whenever anybody went by I would look to see who it was. I was looking for people I had seen before—the man with the hair, the woman. But I saw nobody in that hospital whom I recognized as being on the plane.

I saw nobody I recognized. Not a familiar face. This served to deepen my conviction of the wondrous miracle of my escape. Why me and not others? My mind went to the scene at Calvary when the two thieves were on the cross beside Christ. One called for help and was saved. The other, who did not, was lost.

I reviewed the peace of that moment of escape. The clarity of my thinking, the way I had prayed automatically, the hole in the roof, my ability to get through it. Was I spared so I might tell of His glory? A witness to His presence in the midst of courage?

Suddenly there was a crowd of people in the room. The "team" was back, enough for football, I counted 11.

They really did a job on me. Forty stitches were sewn in my right hand. My left foot was X-rayed. They still didn't find the fracture. I was fed, for the first time. Not bad.

And the team swept off to another room.

Later, the head of this hospital came in to check on me.

"You have an excellent staff," I said to the doctor. He looked about 35.

"We have plenty of people," he replied, "but few are experienced. We need trained people, so we must train them."

He explained the "team" concept. People were doing while learning. They were being trained, perhaps as doctors, nurses, paramedics.

I slept and the night came on.

By this time more facts came to me. Survivors were filling in the story. Monday morning newspapers broke the crash details, including survivor and casualty lists. It was less an airplane crash than a people-crash.

One of the earliest of these first-person accounts appeared in Monday's newspapers (March 28). John Charles Amador, 35, a U.S. Immigration Service hearing officer from Marina del Rey telephoned his father, Charles Amador, a former newsman who then gave the gist of the conversation to the Associated Press.

Amador told his father how he had been sitting on the right side of the plane as it was taxiing for takeoff. He saw the lights of another plane coming down the runway right at him. He put his head between his knees. There was a grinding crash. The plane had split, turbine engines were still screaming, metal flew, there were explosions, flames and acrid smoke. He and his roommate Harry Harper, a pharmacist, realized the plane's nose was tipping toward the ground.

They ran to the rear then started crawling on hands and knees to a break in the fuselage. As they got there, they heard the explosion that rocked the distant KLM plane. Others were trying to escape, debris blocked them, and the heat was so intense it was like being "in an oven." They fought debris and pushed to get to the opening. He reached it and jumped through a rim of fire and smoke to the ground 12 feet below.

Looking around for Harper, Amador found he was not there. He started to go back inside but Captain Grubbs pushed him back. More heroes than we'll ever know.

Stewardess Joan Jackson phoned her fiance John Hackette of Nashville, Tennessee, and told how the Pan Am pilot saw the other jet coming, tried to get out of his way but "it was too late."

A prayerful Jim Naik, of Cupertino, California told the *Los Angeles Times* that he had been blown clear of the plane in the first explosion. He had been trying to free his wife, Elsie, from her seat when the blast came. "Suddenly the plane was completely enveloped in flames," he said. People kept tumbling from the first class compartment above him as he tried to move back in the plane to get Elsie.

Then another fell out of the wreckage and it was his wife. He helped her across the runway. She had a large cut over her eye and head injuries. "I think she's going to pull through," he told the reporter. She did. Naik is financial controller for the Royal Cruise Lines in San Francisco, the organizer of the tour.

The longest distance phone call made was between Tenerife and Hawaii, where one family rejoiced while three others mourned. John and Louisa Combs survived. Their daughter, Susan Hendry of Haleiwa, Hawaii, was able to get a call through Sunday night. She spoke to her mother. Louisa Combs did not want to talk about the crash. She cried a lot over the phone. But Susan determined neither parent was injured critically and that they were feeling "chipper." They expressed a desire to convalesce awhile before returning to Hawaii.

Back on the airfield, the job of clearing the wreckage and removing the bodies and fragments continued for two days.

At first the dead, dying and injured had been spread out on floors as nurses and doctors gave sedatives, stripped away burnt skin, and applied gauze dressings.

Now it was just the dead. No need for nurses and doctors. An empty, tin-roofed hangar was used. Spanish soldiers and police tenderly laid out the charred bodies, in neat rows. Pan Am victims on one side, KLM victims on the other. Here a corpse with clenched fists, there a corpse with outstretched arms reaching for nothing.

A precious mother still held the body of her child protectively.

So badly cremated were some that limbs could not be matched up with bodies. These, together with the corpses, were embalmed and laid into some wooden coffins.

Possessions were brought in from the runway. They too told a story. Comic books, a money clip with 15 dollars, candy, tennis shoes, keys, purses, a doll.

It was the problem of identification which then again required medical personnel. Some 20 pathologists, dentists and photo specialists were recruited.

Heading a three-man team of pathologists for the United States was Dr. William Reals. Dental records provided the chief clues—teeth don't burn.

The spirit of the Tenerife people welled up for the survivors and for the victims.

When the first wounded were assembled in the airport waiting room about 6 P.M. that Sunday night, an immediate appeal went out for doctors and nurses. Within 30 minutes every doctor and nurse contacted had arrived.

Tenerife residents spontaneously rushed in to help in any way they could. Between 6 and 8 P.M. some 200 arrived to give blood; 300 liters of blood was donated that first evening.

Besieged hospitals maintained their "cool." Competence won out over pandemonium. The staffs worked day and night without rest or food. "Dedication beyond our understanding," was the way Pan Am's medical director, Dr. Joseph Constantino, later described it.

On Wednesday, March 30, in a sixteenth century church in La Laguna on the Island of Tenerife a memorial service was held for the dead.

Leading the ecumenical service was Msgr. Franco Gascon, Roman Catholic Bishop of Tenerife Island. Participating were a Dutch Reformed minister from the Netherlands and a rabbi from the local Jewish community. The crossing of religious barriers was symbolized by the yamulke-hatted rabbi speaking under the figure of Christ on the Cross. Crisis again proving a useful leveler of men and traditions.

A representative of King Juan Carlos II of Spain attended as did the Spanish Air Minister and airline officials and investigators from Spain, the Netherlands, and the United States.

The local people sobbed audibly in the church. Cheeks were streamed with tears.

Four surviving stewardesses attended and there were also some next of kin. One was Mary Kay Waters who flew in from San Francisco. Her mother was killed in the crash. Her father, Colonel Waters, died in a Tenerife hospital. Commenting later on the genuine mourning of the local people she said, "It shows that people in the world still care."

There were a few who appeared not to care. The service was continuously disrupted by television technicians flashing bright lights in the face of the mourners, and walking up and down the aisles calling and talking to each other. I found some of this same shabbiness among reporters in the Tenerife hospital.

The only patients I had the privilege to become friendly with were the two young girls in the next room. They were Kim Spocks, 19, and her older married sister, Pam. Their mother had taken them on this "vacation." Now they did not know whether or not she survived. Both girls had severe burns. Later they found out their mother had been lost in the crash.

"At least we know," said Pam.

I would occasionally hop to the door and lean against the corridor wall to chat. I listened to the comments of other survivors.

"Lucky, so lucky," was the comment most frequently heard.

"My anniversary was ruined," said another passenger. "That's the third year in a row that my anniversary has been spoiled by something!" His wife lay seriously injured just a few rooms away.

Some were still re-living the crash and had to keep talking about it.

"My wife and I both hurt our feet jumping. I told her to hang on to me as we moved away. If we are going to go, I said we'll go together."

"Never again," said one man. "I'll never fly again." But he did. He flew out with us just a few days later for home.

"Did you hear that man yelling, 'Let's not panic!'?" A

woman asked another patient in the hallway. "He sounded more panicked than anybody!"

"I was sitting next to the emergency exit," recalled one woman. "It blew off in the first explosion. People climbed right over me to get out." She was sitting with her husband and her 20-year-old daughter. They were with a party of eight from the Los Angeles area. Husband, wife, and daughter jumped safely through that emergency exit. But then her husband went back in the plane to help other members of that party. He never emerged. Heroes. So many heroes.

The misfortune. The good fortune. But so little about the help of God.

I went back to my bed and gazed at that crucifix on the wall.

A man entered my room quietly. He saw me looking at the crucifix.

I said, "Hello. You look like an American."

"I am," he replied. "I'm a Christian missionary. I have lived here quite a few years. My name is Anthony Giordano."

"Have you come across a Ted Younes?" I asked, as I still had no word about my colleague. He had not heard the name.

"What church are you with?" I asked.

"Assembly of God," he replied.

United States Armed Forces were meanwhile preparing to fly the survivors back to America. On Wednesday morning, March 30, a Lockheed C-130 flew from its base at Rhein-Main in West Germany. It made a preliminary pass over the Tenerife airport. Debris still littered the runway. But they found enough space to land. Aboard were cases of medicine and several hundred brown "body bags."

All of the survivors were transported from their various hospitals and clinics by bus and ambulances. I was taken by wheelchair from my room to the bus. There were about 15 others on the bus. I was in my too-small hospital pajamas, carrying a plastic bag containing my bloody clothes. Baggage was a problem for so very few.

When we arrived at the airport, there was that devil's wind again. Chilling. There were two doctors on the bus. I told them I was cold and asked them to help me into my bloody clothes. I was now warmer and more comfortable. I had on cloth "boots" that the hospital gave us, so my feet were comfortable, too.

We were informed that the C-130 would take us over to Las Palmas where a larger Air Force plane, a C-141 would continue our flight to the United States. I was to see Las Palmas after all.

There was a long delay in that bus. Loading the severe cases first, then bureaucratic delays, including detailed consular registration of all the passengers, held up its departure several hours. Strange.

The bus was parked in front of a hangar. It was the morgue hangar. Workers were moving from corpse to corpse trying to match a hand, a finger or a foot. Too awful, too vivid.

And cruel punishment for the survivors to be forced to look upon that scene. Most had friends or loved ones in there.

Finally, the bus moved to the plane where the stretcher cases were already being loaded. There were 39 people on stretchers, 16 ambulatory or close to it, like myself.

Stretchers had to be stacked bunk-style, six high. The rest of us sat along the side.

The door was slammed shut. The engines started. The plane began to taxi. All of us felt it was a tense moment. Like a replay from a few days back. We were going to try again to takeoff from Tenerife Airport.

This time we made it. We were on our way.

Whose failures?
And the Tenerife Control Tower.

Photo by Sjoberg

CHAPTER SEVEN
To Cast the Blame?

Yes, we left for Las Palmas on that jammed hospital plane. But Tenerife's airport problems remained there. Along with the fog that plagued it there was now a pall of guilt for history's biggest air disaster. It had shaken the world, the insurance companies too.

To whom did that guilt belong? The winds blew first one way, then the other.

"Stand by. I will call you for takeoff." The last instructions from Tower Control to the KLM plane, yet, without that next call authorizing takeoff, KLM started its roll down the runway.

Nine minutes of the control tower tapes were analyzed by the authorities. Nothing appeared on them that could answer the question: Why did the KLM captain takeoff? Still to be analyzed were the little black boxes with their recordings of the cockpit chatter among the pilot, copilot and flight engineer.

Teams of investigators from the Netherlands, the United States, Spain and the two airlines began to meticulously reconstruct the events.

At 1:40 P.M. that fatal afternoon, Captain van Zanten set his 747, "The Rhine," down on the runway at Tenerife's Los Rodeos Airport. Four minutes later he radioed the tower that his huge plane was in its parking blocks.

Meanwhile, in the Pan Am 747 still 20 minutes away, Captain Grubbs was studying his Jeppeson route manual, and Pan Am's "T Pages" for more information about Tenerife, the alternate airport. He had never seen it before. From the big blue manual and the company guidebook he found that its runway had a slight slope and that a very tall mountain threatened the approach to its main runway.

Captain Grubbs brought his plane in bumpily at 2:04 P.M. The parking areas were jammed. Ground control directed him to wait on the taxiway. Finally he took his place alongside van Zanten's KLM. Within the hour additional planes had crowded that area—a Scandinavian Airlines 707, a British Airways TriStar, a Sabena 747, at least two Sterling Airlines jets from Denmark, and a couple of Spanish charter planes.

During the waiting that followed, the KLM captain studied his full load. His refueling would ordinarily be done at Las Palmas, but, according to Tenerife airport authorities, the Dutch captain thought that refueling later would increase the delay for his return flight back to Amsterdam. He ordered the fuel.

When Pan Am Copilot Bragg heard this, he initiated voice contact with van Zanten asking how long his refueling would take. "About 35 minutes" was the reply. This was when Bragg left the cockpit to pace off the distance between the KLM plane and the next plane, accompanied by his flight engineer.

The result: negative. The Pan Am plane would have to await the KLM's refueling despite the fact that Las Palmas airport had just been reopened. They were blocked from leaving by the Dutchman's jet.

At 4:57 P.M., the refueling completed, the KLM captain radioed for ground clearance—a standard first step in which basic altitude and radio contact requirements are given. Tower Control gave the KLM permission to begin taxiing, the start of the fateful nine-minute period.

The KLM plane was told to proceed right up the main runway and turn around, preparatory to takeoff. Three minutes later, the Pan Am captain was given the same clearance to taxi up the same runway but to turn left at the third ramp.

When the Dutch aircraft reached the end of the runway, control tower tapes record a clear instruction by the tower to hold. The exact words on the tape were: "Stand by. I will call you for takeoff."

But KLM did not stand by. Van Zanten opened his throttles.

So confident in their crack pilot were the KLM investigators that they refused to accept the possibility that he could have taken off without proper clearance. It was suggested that the air controllers may not have spoken English well. So the two air controllers and their assistants who were in the tower at the time were interviewed.

"Textbook English" was the way an observer described the way the tower staff spoke the universal language of air traffic. One report that the tower personnel was watching a televised soccer match between Spain and Hungary at the time could likewise not be proved.

It was established that the control tower staff had followed the correct procedures throughout.

Pan Am Captain Grubbs' actions then came under criticism, especially from KLM officials. Instructions from the tower were that he should turn off at the third exit. There were four. These were marked on the charts as C-1 through C-4. Why did he pass C-3 and head for C-4?

Pan Am officials insisted that Captain Grubbs was instructed to take "the third exit on the left." C-1 was inactive, blocked by parked planes so it could not be counted. Furthermore, the one marked C-3 would require a difficult 150-degree turn. It was reasonable, they contended that C-4, the third available exit and properly angled, was the proper exit.

It was the exit Captain Grubbs was looking at but never reached. Should Grubbs have risked the narrow C-3, even though angled?

Still the fact remained that the KLM pilot should never have taken off without clearance. Equally puzzling was why two seasoned pilots of "heavies" would attempt their flights at all with such poor ground visibility. According to the Associated Press, Franz van Rejsen, head of the Dutch Civil Aviation Authority team of investigators, admitted the KLM pilot had been given preliminary clearance for takeoff but not final clearance. "But the KLM started, which is not in accordance with normal procedure," he stated. "We presume there was a misunderstanding in the KLM cockpit regarding the position of the Pan Am plane on the runway."

Had the KLM captain mistaken his instructions?

Had static cut off some words, giving him a mistaken understanding of what tower was saying?

Had he taken matters into his own hands because of impatience at the lengthy delay and judged the Pan Am position wrongly? Had he been tempted by a momentary "hole" in the ground fog?

Those who knew the reliability of Captain van Zanten called the third and fourth alternatives unthinkable.

As for a static-garbled Tower Control message, "Clipper 1736, report clear of runway." Did it come to him as "Clipper 1736 *reports* clear of runway"? One little 's' difference?

Or it might have been the Pan Am reply, "We'll report when clear of runway" came over to his ears as "We report clear of runway."

Still another possibility—when the tower asked Pan Am to report when clear of runway, the answer was "Roger, we will report when we are clear." Could the final *three* words have been the only ones heard through static in the KLM cockpit?

Spanish officials immediately impounded the flight recorders which recorded pilot conversations in the cockpits both internal and over the air. On Wednesday, March 30, without any statement regarding their contents, it was agreed to release these flight recorders to the team of investigators.

By agreement of both Dutch and American officials, the tapes were flown to Washington for analysis by a joint group including Pan Am and KLM crew members who could identify the voices.

Could it happen again? The answer is a qualified "yes," according to the International Federation of Airline Pilots Associations. They give Boston's Logan Airport a "black star," indicating deficient safety conditions.

The condition that was signaled out in particular was the Logan Airport rule, requiring planes to takeoff at night at times in the face of incoming aircraft on the same runway—a rule imposed because of noise abatement efforts. Los Angeles has a similar noise abatement ruling making for an accident waiting to happen.

A spokesman for the Federal Aviation Administration immediately disagreed with the pilots' group, saying that only about 12 flights a night are affected by the rule in Boston.

At Tenerife, it took only two flights.

Actually, it has happened before. In 1972, at Chicago's O'Hare Airport, a plane that was taking off crashed into another plane taxiing across the runway in foggy weather. Ten were killed.

Only 26 airports in the world have the "black star." Tenerife was not yet listed. However, because of the frequent fog, fierce winds, that particular mountain and the runway, it is a problem field. On March 29, an editorial appeared in the local newspaper, "If it turns out that the airport was operating as it should and that the catastrophe was due to human error, it will not obscure the fact that Los Rodeos has built up an appalling reputation."

During the past 21 years, this Tenerife airport was the site of six other accidents killing a total of 252 people. The largest was the accident on December 3, 1972 when a chartered Spanish Convair 990 was caught by a sudden cross-wind on takeoff. It flipped over and exploded, killing all 155 German tourists aboard. In another incident, the president of Iberia escaped from the crash of a Spanish National Airline plane. Four were killed in that one.

Tenerife's fog problem is compounded by the existence of two sets of visibility rules. One standard applies to United States planes. It sets required visibility to be at least 500 meters (547 yards), as spelled out by the Federal Aviation Administration.

The other standard, set by the Spanish government and applying to all except U.S. planes, sets required visibility to be at 250 meters, or only half again. That's pretty short for jets moving 200 miles per hour on takeoff.

The Dutch government's chief investigator, Franz van Rejsen, said that visibility was 300 meters at the time of our crash. Earlier a Spanish official had said 500 meters. I see how this discrepancy could exist because it changed from moment to moment as the wind blew. It all depended on when and where you were.

At any rate, the double standard at Tenerife explains why Captain Grubbs was planning to wait for improvement when our jetliner reached its takeoff position. The KLM pilot was obviously not even considering this.

I have not come away from the Tenerife crash bitter about the two pilots or the control tower. Nor do I have a fear of flying.

I see the Hand of God involved in my rescue. Why should I ever be afraid again?

MURPHY'S LAW

And there have been too many "what if's" to conceive that a tragedy of this configuration could ever happen again. It would not have occurred if any single one of these "what if's" were missing:

- What if the delay had not occurred in Los Angeles?

- What if the bomb had not been thrown in Las Palmas?
- What if the caller had not "hoaxed" a second bomb?
- What if the *Golden Odyssey* had come for us?
- What if the fog had not blown in to obstruct KLM's view of us down the runway?
- What if it had been still worse to prevent a try?
- What if the KLM plane had not refueled and blocked our path in order to takeoff first?
- What if the space between planes had not been too small?
- What if KLM had heard better?
- What if Grubbs could have gotten off the runway at C-3?
- What if van Zanten could have lifted over us without the extra fuel load?

On and on. . . .

Fate strung every one of these beads to make the terror at Tenerife necklace. It took every one of these beads to string the crash.

I am thoroughly confident in the safety of commercial flying. I shall continue to fly. It is statistically 10 times safer than driving your car.

In 1976, the United States airlines had the fewest accidents in its history and the lowest number of fatalities in 20 years, this in the face of an all-time high 2.5 billion miles logged and a record 220 million passengers.

The National Transportation and Safety Board records show that, until the Canary Islands crash, no fatal accident involving a United States charter flight had occurred since 1970. They also show that airlines registered in the United States are four times safer than the world average.

The 747 has paced this safety record. When they were first certified for flight in December, 1969, insurance experts extrapolated their statistics and predicted there would be two disastrous crashes within the 747's first 18 months of operation. There were two crashes, but it took nearly five years to happen:

On May 20, 1974, a Lufthansa 747 crashed on takeoff at Nairobi, Kenya. There were 59 dead.

On May 19, 1976, an Iranian Air Force 747 broke apart above Huete, Spain. Seventeen died.

These were the only two fatal accidents involving the 747 until Tenerife.

There are 298 747's in service, the most recent having been named the "Charles Lindbergh" honoring the 50th anniversary of his flight to Paris.

Tenerife's death toll of 581 far exceeded any airline disaster in the past. Prior to that, the worst one took place on March 3, 1974 when a Turkish DC-10 crashed at Ermenonville, France, just outside of Paris, with 346 dead.

Some two and a half years later, two airplanes collided in midair near Zagreb, Yugoslavia, a British Airways Trident and a chartered Yugoslavian airliner. That was on September 10, 1976. Dead: 176.

The Pan Am survivors at Tenerife were too grateful for their escape to take part in the leveling of blame. I heard nothing but praise for the Captain and crew.

The stewardesses that had appeared impersonal and curt on the flight over the Atlantic certainly "came alive" in the emergency. Several had dashed back into the flames to help more people and never emerged. First-class girls indeed.

Captain Grubbs admitted that his first reaction was one of intense remorse at having the disaster befall his plane, but in his heart he felt he was not to blame. When he was airlifted out, Captain Grubbs was quoted by the Spanish news agency "Europa Press" as saying, "I have a tranquil conscience about my performance in the accident. I am convinced that I maneuvered the plane skillfully and carried out the instructions the control tower gave me."

Damage suits have been filed. International conventions under the Warsaw Treaty limit the airline's liability to their own passengers. KLM will be able to claim a liability limit of 11,700 pounds sterling under the 1955 Hague protocol to the treaty. Pan Am will be liable up to $75,000 per passenger under the terms of the 1965 Montreal agreement modifying the treaty. These limits would not hold if "willful misconduct" is proved. It is expected that the lawyers for Pan Am passengers will attempt to prove KLM negligent and lawyers for KLM passengers will attempt to prove Pan Am negligent.

An advertisement was halted in the Netherlands, too. It featured Captain Veldhuyzen van Zanten, their chief jet instructor. In fact, a KLM executive on hearing a KLM plane was down in the Canary Islands, ordered that Captain van Zanten be located and sent to the crash site to investigate! But he turned out to be the downed pilot.

It is a comforting thought to know that crashes like that at Canary Islands trigger investigations which can then lead to improved air safety.

Since the O'Hare ground collision in 1972, nine large airports have installed equipment which gives air traffic controllers a ground picture of what is happening on runways and ramps. The tragedy is it hasn't been installed at more airports, especially ones like Tenerife where ground fog is such a problem.

Data from the Canary Islands and other major crashes are sifted by pilots, controllers, aircraft manufacturers, airlines, flight attendants and government agencies to make flying tomorrow even safer than today.

I have flown over 10,000 miles since the crash and up to the time of this writing, including the flight back to California, a round-trip to Hawaii, to Phoenix and elsewhere. It has not occurred to me to pause and be concerned.

In the short time it takes to read this book, a million people have flown from here to there,—economically, quickly, safely. Flying is safe—that's the short and the long of it. So I prefer to think of the larger Hand. The Hand that guides my hands, your hands.

"GOTT DAM!" The final words of the KLM captain. "God damnit!" He and every wonderful person in his plane perished.

There were many God-loving people on that plane. All we can say from this human point of vantage is that these are receiving their great rewards in Heaven right now. Rewards far better than we earthly survivors know.

If you had a choice of a flight, would you choose a plane of God-blessers or the other? It is not usually that black or white a choice, it is often gray. But, if you put yourself in God's Hand, what is best for you always happens.

There has been proof to me of that not only in the Canary Islands escape, but in other accidents I have survived. It gets down to the fundamentals of Christianity. If you are a Christian all the way, fear has no place to reside in you. Fear separates you from our Lord. It is the opposite of faith.

Remember the bumper sticker that has been around a lot lately? "If you feel separated from God, you know who moved."

Fearlessness is not rashness. You need always to use God-given intelligence. It is through that intelligence that God may "speak" to us. It may come in the form of intuition, inspiration, discrimination, judgment, hunch, knowledge and many others.

Remember Paul and Floy Heck? Floy is the one who hurt her leg when jumping from the plane. She became immobilized and could not move away from the burning fuselage. She called on Jesus for help and immediately was able to crawl to safety.

Just that morning her husband Paul had reviewed with her, flying over the Atlantic, exactly what to do in case of emergency—how to escape over the wing.

A few hours later when that emergency exploded upon

them, that morning's "intelligence briefing" made a difference. At first, Floy just sat there, then she remembered that discussion when Paul yelled, "Come on!" They headed immediately for that exit. A curtain of flames blocked their way. He made a sweeping motion—and the flame was pushed aside. . . .

She continued to pray in the ambulance. In it was a girl crying, "I know my leg is gone." Another was moaning, "Oh God, I can't stand it." They all prayed together. Their prayers worked.

Seconds count. In an emergency, God moves you in the right direction for survival. Unless . . . One of those "unlesses" is fear. God cannot move you if you lock yourself to fear.

Sometimes the devil knows bits of the future too. But he never knows it all.

Newspapers reported that a Duke University freshman, Lee Fried, wrote a number of predictions on paper cards on March 21 and brought them to the president of the university, Terry Sanford. The Duke community relations director was present, too. They both agreed to sign the back of the cards before they were put in an envelope and sealed with wax. Sanford locked the envelopes in his desk, and put the key in a box that had a combination lock.

On March 29, a day after the Canary Islands headlines appeared, the envelope was opened in front of a television audience. His prediction read, "583 Die in Collision of 747's in Worst Disaster in Aviation History." The Monday morning edition of the *Raleigh News and Observer* reads, "Worst Air Disaster In History."

Trick? Of the devil? Coincidence? Maybe.

The Bible is full of *never-miss* prophecies. Some of those prophecies are now coming true in modern history.

Fried's prediction may yet prove to be exactly accurate. A few days after the Canary Islands disaster, on April 1,

Jack Gillen, a guest on Dick Syatt's radio talk show, in Dallas, told 300,000 listeners that an airliner would crash on April 4 near Atlanta. That prediction became a tragic truth, when on that very day, a Southern Airways DC-9 crashed in New Hope, Georgia, not far from Atlanta while trying to make an emergency landing on a highway. Seventy were killed.

Why glimpses of the future come to people about some things and not to others remain a mystery. One of the characteristics of the coming Antichrist will be his psychic-phenomenon signs and wonders. Where were these coming from? You be the judge.

If your life is a continuous worship of the Lord, He may speak to you and you will know. "My sheep hear My voice."

I am living proof of that.

I know I am watched over by God, taken care of by God. I am nobody special, yet somebody special to Him.

Have you a fear of flying? Then I say read "The Word." Erase every reason why you have not read the Bible recently and pick it up and begin reading it.

This is a real book. Nonfiction. Archeologists are discovering proof after proof of the Bible's authenticity; even finding parts of Noah's huge ark 10,000 feet high, buried in the snow and ice of Mt. Ararat in Turkey, exactly as the Old Testament recounts.

I did not have a moment of fear at Tenerife. Surrounded by white, hot metal, searing flames, and flying debris I moved calmly—albeit in superhuman ways. Others sat transfixed by fear, in effect, letting fear separate themselves from God's help.

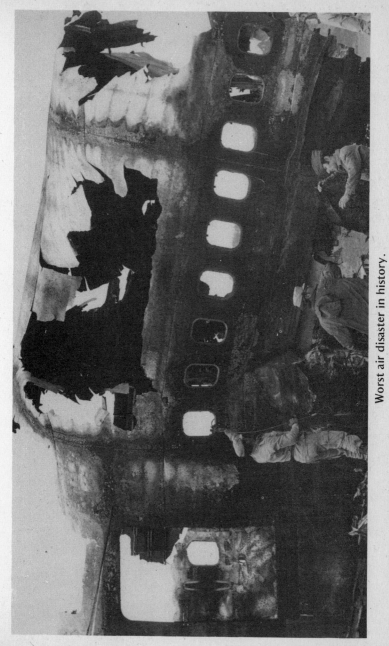

Worst air disaster in history.

Photo: Henri Bureau/Sygma

Mario "Ham" Tyzbir,
Laguna Hills, Calif.

CHAPTER EIGHT
Chosen to Return

And so we were at last all crammed onto the smaller C-130 for that flight over to Las Palmas where we would transfer to a bigger bird.

The Lockheed C-141 Starlifter which we were to fly back home in was too big to land on the damaged runway at Tenerife. And so this big transport had to wait for us over at Las Palmas, a 30 minute hop away.

I was glad it was to be a short flight over to the Las Palmas airport because we were terribly crowded on that C-130. Originally, they were going to make two trips with the C-130 but the second trip might have got socked in with that late afternoon fog. Sound familiar? So we were doing it in one trip—squeezed in and stacked up.

The survivors on the lower-stretcher tier got every vibration in that plane. One was Captain Grubbs, directly opposite my bench seat. He was one who was particularly glad when that shaking half hour flight was over. When you are injured and burned it is like having every nerve end cruelly exposed.

At Las Palmas, the transfer was made efficiently—first the ambulatory people, then those on stretchers.

We were airborne again, heading westward this time across the lonely Atlantic. What a pitiful remnant we were from the two big airplane loads which had started out.

The C-141 was configured for medical evacuation. There was much more space for stretchers, so they were stacked in tiers of only three or four. The rest of us had regular seats, but we were facing backwards. Like the bus standing by the terrible hangar morgue, this seemed to be symbolic of some underlying imperative that we "look back" at what had happened that we might learn and teach others.

The bodies of those who had been identified needed to be evacuated too. A few days after our departure the wooden coffins bearing the KLM dead would be flown out. But the brown wooden boxes bearing the Pan Am dead could not leave Tenerife until early the following week. They were flown in cargo jets to Delaware's Dover Air Force Base.

Many personal experiences were able to be shared on the C-141 trip that could not be told before. We were all in one plane. We had time. We had space to shuffle around, if we were physically able. My left foot was still quite swollen and extremely painful when the slightest weight was put on it.

But a few others moved about and exchanged information.

"They told me my wife was dead," said one man. "The next day they said she was alive. I did not know what to believe until I saw her with my own eyes. There she was—alive!"

This recalled the identification problems in those first few hours after the crash. It was more important for the medical teams to sort out the people according to their medical urgencies than family-wise. Some were marked for surgery, some for treatment of shock, some for burns, others for cuts, broken bones. American names were not familiar to the Canary Islanders. They wrote down identifications based on the phonetic sound or from papers which, in some cases, confused proper identification.

Thanks largely to an American medical student who was at the general hospital, the task of names was beginning to get straightened out by the morning following the crash. Steven Wrigly of Pleasantville, New Jersey rushed back and forth between hospitals, sorting out patients' names and relationships. It cut down a lot of anxiety for those who had gotten separated and didn't know what had happened to their traveling partners.

There was one moment of humor in this time of finding out names and caring of the hurt. After the crash, a woman in the assembly room kept asking for "my red handbag." Amid such cries of "Don't cut off my legs," "Send me home to my son," and "Where's my husband—I want my husband," this lady was persistently calling for "my red handbag." In spite of their strained bodies and minds, people began automatically looking for that bag. So, here she was now enroute home, showing off that same red handbag. And I thought how good, how humorous.

Some passengers had boarded the C-130 reluctantly. But the Tenerife medical service was so full and at such a high level of expertise. "If I ever crash again," said one passenger, "I hope it's in the Canary Islands." It was the highest honor they could be paid.

Lt. Colonel James K. Slaton headed a medical team rushed from its U.S. Air Force base at Torrejon, Spain. "The Tenerife doctors stabilized their patients very quickly," he said. "They deserve nothing but praise."

We found out during the flight back that the Tenerife medical staff had been augmented by wonderful volunteers. A vacationing English surgeon rushed in to help, as did a West German anesthetist. A number of women in the islands' British community also volunteered.

As we flew west racing with the sun, our day was a long one. Starlifter was an Air Force medical crew consisting of two doctors and two nurses. They administered pain medication, changed dressings and did all they could to make both stretcher and ambulatory passengers comfortable.

Several survivors were not on our plane. One stewardess

was still hospitalized at Tenerife. Another stewardess had already left the island. Several others had stayed on intending to go to Madrid, Spain. One survivor had not been transferred in Las Palmas from the C-130 and we learned later that this person had died, while in a Las Palmas hospital, of a ruptured spleen.

Flying back over the Atlantic, we lost one more of our dear people from burns. She was Isabelle Lord of Long Beach, California. She was 46 and a former Tampa, Florida school teacher who had moved to Long Beach to become a college librarian.

The doctors and nurses worked feverishly on the seriously hurt all night long. Some of the rest of us talked.

Certain things stuck in people's minds: The brave stewardess that was inflating a life raft when an explosion decapitated her. People who were reluctant to jump. "I had to physically push them," said architect John Combs of Hawaii. And the heat: "I felt like I was roasting."

What stuck out in my mind was God's miraculous rescue. Then why the conversation on the flames, the blood, the gore, the anguish? Why not on the joy of rescue?

That plane should have resounded with exultation to the Lord all the way back.

Some of it was. A woman sitting next to me had dragged her injured husband several hundred yards away from the exploding wreckage.

"Your husband must be slight of build," she was told.

"No. In fact, he's a lot larger than I am."

"Then you must be a very strong woman."

She replied, simply "Not really."

"Then how could you have physically moved your husband as you did?"

"I don't know. It was as if something or someone had helped me."

Someone, indeed. . . .

Praise the Lord, I whispered, wishing I could shout it.

I still had no news about Ted Younes. He was not on that trip back, but he could have been too badly injured to move. Nobody seemed to know about Ted.

As night fell, we were informed that we would be making two stops on the way to California. The first would be at McGuire Air Force Base in New Jersey. There, 10 survivors who were either residents of the East Coast or most seriously injured would leave the plane.

The second stop would be at Kelly Air Force Base where the most seriously burned would deplane for the Army Burn Unit in San Antonio.

The final destination would be El Toro Marine Air Base in California.

"Relatives are being informed of your estimated time of arrival at all stops and final destination," it was announced.

That was a relief. My mother knew I was on my way home.

The touchdown at McGuire in New Jersey was at 1:00 A.M., Wednesday EST. The husband of the woman next to me was to leave the plane here because of the seriousness of his injuries. She looked worried as she prepared to leave. "I don't know anybody on the East Coast," she said to me as we were about to land. "And I have no money."

"I'm sure they will take complete care of you," I assured her.

She still seemed concerned, so I reached into my wallet and took out a 20 dollar bill.

"Oh, no," she said, "not that much. Maybe just some small change." But I insisted she have more. She was so grateful. She seemed to feel there might be a difference in the way we would be treated now.

In all, 10 left the plane here, including Captain Grubbs.

Crowds lined the area where we had parked. There were many ambulances, more ambulances than passengers who left the plane. We found out later that some 200 volunteer members of the Burlington County Emergency Medical

Service had come to the air base. Pan Am officials had been informed that military vehicles would not be available. Also, a larger number had been expected to deplane.

Furthermore, an inaccurate arrival time had been announced. The volunteers had started assembling at 3:00 P.M. the previous afternoon. A "hurry up and wait" situation.

At about 2:00 A.M., the 10 deplaning passengers were aboard military vehicles. The volunteers waited, expecting more to leave the plane. At 2:30 A.M., nearly 12 hours after some of them had arrived, they were told their services would not be needed. The volunteers were furious—and understandably so. A breakdown in communications had caused them loss of time and energy.

I want to say "Thank you" here and now to those Burlington County volunteers. All of us aboard appreciated their effort.

It was a sleepy droning lot to Kelly Air Force Base. We landed just before 7:00 A.M.

"How was your flight?" asked a boarding officer at Kelly.

"Not exactly jolly," replied Edward Hess, a 39-year-old food broker from Phoenix. "There wasn't much to joke about."

His hands were throbbing as he left the plane to have his serious burns treated. His wife Mary, 36, also left here for treatment at the Army Burn Unit. A total of 14 survivors, 12 on stretchers, left us at Kelly.

Burn patients knew that they would have to spend at least one day for every one percent of their body which had burned. Treatment would include protection against the high danger of infection, the maintenance of body fluid levels, and a high caloric food intake to prevent weight loss.

I watched as the 12 stretcher cases, covered with bandages and blankets, were carried out the huge rear cargo doors which our seats were facing. They also carried off the lady who had died on the flight.

Those 12, I knew, were in a painful fight for their lives. Some had nearly half of their body covered with burns. Some would need skin grafts to replace tissue that had been totally destroyed.

A person under 40 is estimated by doctors to have a 50 percent chance for survival when half the body is covered with second- or third-degree burns. These odds decreased with increasing age. The three oldest ranged in ages from 55 to 75.

We prayed for their recovery.

They were in competent hands. The Brooke Army Medical Center in San Antonio has in it the Institute for Surgical Research. It was started during the Vietnam war, specializing in care of the seriously burned. It has the reputation of being one of the best in the world in this field.

It was while waiting in this Texas airport that I learned for the first time that Ted Younes had not survived. By this time I had braced for this possibility, but it was still a bitter shock. A young man like that, with such promise ahead of him. I prayed that his family might be given the strength and protection they now needed.

Morticians working in Tenerife hangar morgue.
The view from the bus.

CHAPTER NINE
Enshrining of the Heroes

At last we took off on the final leg of our flight.

My injured foot had been throbbing all the way from the Canary Islands. Just the weight of it on the floor was unbearable. Now, however, there was more room and they put a chair in front of me so I could keep my foot elevated. It helped.

There were just 26 of us left aboard. Steering for El Toro Marine Air Base 40 miles east of Los Angeles. It was about a four-hour flight but due to the time change, we would be arriving at 10:00 A.M. The strung-out flight from Tenerife seemed like it would never end.

I thought again about Ted. That completed the circle. People in front of me, to my left, to my right, and behind me had died.

Why were we, the survivors, spared?

I wondered if it might have a reason. Voices to tell of God's help in the midst of chaos.

The accident resulted from human error. But God was quickly on the scene and into the fire. He provided an escape route for me, one of His own children, and for others.

I resolved while flying that lonely journey home to tell of His wonderful love. . . .

Whatever your need, circumstances or wherever you are,

He is there! All He asks is that you reach out, receive and stand upon His Word!

I looked out of the window. Toy cars raced along highway ribbons. Smoke rose from industrial buildings. Everything was the same. They were not listening.

We were over California and on our landing approach.

Below, relatives and newsmen stood silently along the runway in front of the control tower. Hardly a word was spoken as they watched the giant silver plane touch the ground at 10:18 A.M.

Then there was loosed all pandemonium. Reporters from every television, radio station and newspaper must have been there. This had been the starting point for most on the ill-fated trip—California. I was in no condition to be a vibrant witness but others were. Duane and Bonnie McCreery standing outside were approached by the television news reporters from all around the country. When asked for reaction to the survival of her parents who were on board, Bonnie exclaimed, "Praise the Lord! We are so thankful they are alive and coming back."

Hardly a word was spoken inside the big C-141 as the rear doors were opened. Ambulances quietly positioned themselves.

Doctors went aboard first to check passengers.

Newsmen, spectators and families squeezed closer to the fence to get a better view. The stretchers began to be carried off. A hovering helicopter broke the silence.

Pam and Kim, my two "neighbors" at the Tenerife hospital, were met by a private jet and whisked right off. That gave a few of the newspapers a human interest angle. But human interest was the name of the game at El Toro that Wednesday morning.

My mother and sister were out there. I did not see them but they saw me carried off on a stretcher and placed in an ambulance.

Lying on my back, all I could see was the California sky.

It was a bright sunny day. Super! A cool wind whipped up but it was different than the ill wind of Tenerife.

In the ambulance was a nurse and one other survivor. I was allowed to sit on a side seat. The survivor was my new friend, John Combs of Hawaii. A wonderful man.

We were taken to the Burn Treatment Center of the University of California at Irvine (UCI), along with 10 or 12 other survivors. Some were taken to the University of Southern California Medical Center in Los Angeles, and still others to Saddleback Community Hospital in Laguna.

At UCI I was taken to the Orthopedic section. There my foot was X-rayed, where at last it was discovered it had been broken. My severely cut hands were healing.

I was immediately prepared for surgery and an operation was performed on my left foot, inserting pins into the small bones to relocate them into their normal position. Now, I had to learn to use crutches.

Medical attention was the best that money could buy. But whose money?

When we left the Tenerife hospital not a penny changed hands. All offers of payment were politely refused.

Leaving the UCI hospital about a week later I decided to ask about the bill.

"Money has not been mentioned so far, doctor, I would like to know how much I owe you."

"Pan Am is footing the bill," was his reply. That was reassuring.

So there was no crash expense. The cost of the airline disaster, at least to survivors, would have to be measured in other ways.

Back at Tenerife 58 million dollars worth of airplanes were lying there dead, too. Inconsequential when measured against the hurting people and families of the lost.

But it was great to be home, albeit on crutches. My mother made a pretty good nurse. All that experience with her mine-injured husband now came in handy with her son, a survivor of the world's greatest air disaster.

She showed me the Wednesday, March 30 edition of newspapers covering my return. I told her how I felt God may have spared me, to be able to tell about it.

"If that is your calling, Norman," she replied, "then you must do it."

In reading the newspapers and magazine stories I was glad to see there was beginning to be some mention of credit to the Lord.

Captain Grubbs was quoted as saying it was "a miracle" that anyone was saved. That comes pretty close.

A woman said, "It was like the Hindenburg blowing up. It was a terrible sight. I said 'Jesus, help me,' and He did."

One man, whom I never before had heard credit the Lord, was quoted in the newspapers as admitting the position of his seat was a "Godsend."

Maybe hindsight would be giving others a clearer view of the Divine aspects of their survival.

A news item told of one survivor, who "towed" his seatmate to safety, receiving a heroism award. His seatmate said "You saved my life," he had replied. "I owe you one."

The story that appeared in the April 26 *Star*, a tabloid weekly, was told by Edward Hess, the man who helped rescue his wife Mary. She was the woman who received "a push from the rear." According to Hess, "Nobody followed her out. Whoever helped her escape didn't get out."

Now, if as I suspect that push was from an angel of the Lord, he is out OK.

It was not easy to get around yet. Crutches are not as efficient as legs. Friday the thirteenth of May was to be my lucky day when the pins would come out.

Perhaps after that date, opportunities would come for me to speak out if it pleased God.

Those opportunities were to come sooner.

On Wednesday, April 27, a mass funeral was held for

114 victims who could not be identified, exactly one month after the crash, lined up in rows of white burial vaults in a special location of Los Angeles' Westminster Memorial Park. A single red rose was laid atop each vault. The Orange County location had been selected for the mass burial.

Pan Am provided transportation for the victims' survivors to attend and for the cost of the services.

The sky was partly cloudy and several hundred people had gathered at a designated area separated by a white tape from the vaults.

Among them were many of my fellow survivors. We embraced. We hugged. There were tears. We now felt so close to each other. Certainly closer than if we had spent two weeks together on the *Golden Odyssey.*

This odyssey, though pained, was more meaningful than a thousand cruises.

I recognized quite a few, including my hospital room neighbors Pam and Kim. Their mother was one of those beneath a red rose.

Now some 1,500 persons had gathered and the service began.

References were made to the bon voyages said a month ago and the good-byes being said now, "for the final time." Hope was expressed that the mourners would take the best from the lives of the deceased, "enshrining them in yours."

The names were intoned one by one.

Pam and Kim looked at each other. Their mother's name had not been mentioned. It was a shaking experience for both of them. There were tears on their faces when they abruptly left.

The burial vaults then began to be lowered into the mass grave. People drove away.

I thought about the hurt that Pam and Kim felt when their mother's name went unmentioned. I mention it now:

MARGARET FOX

When I left that memorial service, I knew that the

curtain had fallen on the dead and that now the spotlight must be on the living. That those deaths shall not have been in vain.

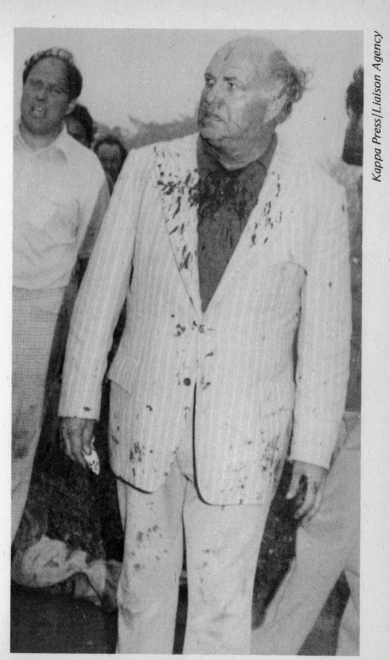

Norman Williams at Tenerife.

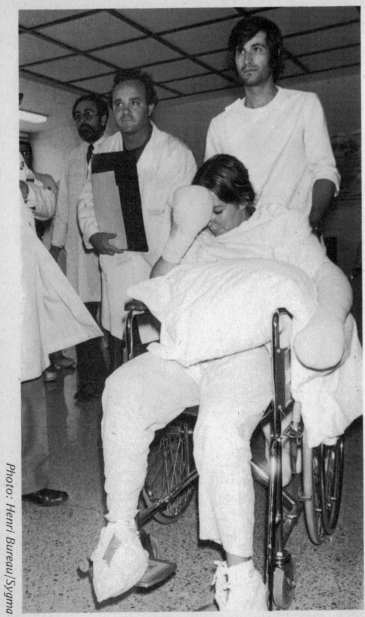

Photo: Henri Bureau/Sygma

The people were so brave.
The medical people so wonderful.

CHAPTER TEN
Anatomy of Disasters

Disasters make violent catalysts to stir the secret place down where man really lives. They are separators for both men and women—bringing out their worst or best. How would you react in the face of panic and death? Few are allowed to face the test.

Earthquakes, typhoons, plagues, fires, floods, war, crashes and ship disasters stretch man's character to its outer limits. But the conditions and values of the total society also play a part. Back in an era when chivalry and principles were at a premium one such test came.

The unsinkable superliner Titanic sunk! Unlike the instant carnage from Pan Am and KLM planes colliding, there were a few hours for the Titanic's passengers to contemplate their fate. Every survivor came back to tell a heartwarming story of the elegance of character displayed by those who went down with the ship.

Gentlemen gave up their life jackets and lifeboats to the ladies and children. And as they did so, they helped swing away their only link to life. The age of chivalry was in full and fragrant blossom. The ship's band and the doomed men joined in singing stirring hymns as the waters rose to consume them. Nothing is so beautiful as people at their loftiest. People: the highest product of a living God, "made in our image."

Why today have we begun to exalt the cowardly, the cheap and the base in man?

On a more recent Saturday night fire roared through the Beverly Hills Supper Club in Southgate, Kentucky, across the Ohio River from Cincinnati. One hundred and sixty died.

It was the largest loss of human life by fire in the United States since a similar nightclub fire in Boston over 40 years before, and the largest disaster on earth since Tenerife. Only 60 days had passed.

In the aftermath of that Kentucky fire were again hundreds of unhurt survivors and injured survivors. Scores of identified corpses and unidentified corpses. Here again the unidentified bodies were placed in neat rows—reminiscent of the Tenerife hangar.

Inlcuded also in the aftermath of the fire were the repercussions and recriminations: Who or what was to blame?

Among the survivors there were both the tales of horror and, yes, cowardice, courage, selfishness and valor. There were the screams, the dying curses, the trampling, the heat.

To the time of this writing, the reasons for that fire and the difficulty of escape have not been determined.

Tenerife survivors read newspaper accounts of that Kentucky disaster with mixed feelings.

"I don't want to hear about it."

"I know what they must have gone through."

"Fate?"

My own reaction was to wonder if there had been any miraculous escapes like mine. Why were there reports of panic and selfishness by some in their hour of need? Were there any Christians in that smoky nightclub, drinking and listening to double-meaning jokes? Were there any who prayed and stood on His Word? I hoped some had.

Catastrophes affect the lives of people who emerge from them, whether in Kentucky or Tenerife. I was beginning to see a bit of change in my life.

Were we all changing?

One of the researchers for this book called a survivor a few months after the crash, and asked, "Has Tenerife changed your life?"

The reply was, "I am not saying anything. You are only trying to make money out of this story. I'm sick of reporters."

Again a question: "How might the survivors contribute to the future welfare of humanity?"

The reply: "Why should I line your pockets?"

"Can we get together and discuss any changes in your philosophy of life?" was asked.

The answer, "No."

End of conversation.

The person was not that way before Tenerife. The researcher checked with people who had known this person well. Maybe some rudeness by reporters at Tenerife brought about bitterness. Maybe the flames of the Tenerife crash left memories too terrible to bear. We may never know.

It is difficult to speak to some of the survivors today and get them to see themselves objectively. Yet the changes are there. It is impossible to go through such an experience and not be affected by it.

Marianne Tyler, staff writer for the *Los Angeles Herald-Examiner,* interviewed two couples about eight weeks after the crash. Her May 24 story reflects both reticence to talk and a vivid recollection of every detail. I gather from it that both couples have a renewed zest for life. One of the couples, Harold and Grace McGowan, are in their mid-70s. They were members of the group from Leisure World.

Harold McGowan has been living a "bachelor's life," waiting for the day when his wife is released from the hospital so they can go about their activities. They are, in his words, "just so glad to be alive." He is a golfer and has temporarily given up playing in order to visit his wife in the hospital at least twice a day. She has had to have a skin graft on her badly lacerated foot. They have been married 52 wonderful years. He has recovered completely from his physical injuries—cuts, bruises, and second-degree burns.

But neither have recovered completely from memories of the disaster. "It's on my mind a lot," Harold says. He does not sleep as well as he used to. Grace still has nightmares.

Harold was the survivor who caught his trousers on some jagged metal while going over the side of the fuselage. He dangled there in peril of his life until freed by another passenger. His wife jumped out behind him. Harold remembered to take pills he carries for a heart condition as he was crawling away from the wreck. Fortunately, he and his wife, together with the couple they were traveling with, were all driven away in the same ambulance.

The Hecks were not immediately that fortunate. They got lost once outside the wreck. They went off different parts of the wing and did not see each other again until the C-130 departure from Tenerife. The Hecks experienced wonderful strengthening of family ties like the McGowans. Harold McGowan felt a new surge of warmth for his entire family. The Tenerife experience for him was in his words, it "made us all a little closer."

The Hecks experienced a rebirth of deeper family ties and love for God. Floy said, "Somehow that fiery collision has drawn us nearer to God and each other."

Neither family feel any bitterness about what they have been put through. But all the scars of the memory will never be erased.

The trick is to make use of those memories toward a better life and Paul Heck seems to be doing just that. He realizes how strong his urge to live really is. His memory of beating aside the flames that blocked his way convinces him that "no matter how adverse future conditions, I'll fight through it."

Floy Heck remembers the way she sat stunned until her husband spurred her into action. Other passengers, including their dear friends Karl and Lorraine Larson across the aisle, sat as if they were frozen, "immobile and glassy-eyed like rows of figures in a wax museum." *By fearing it was the end,* it became the end.

Have we learned anything about fear? Have we learned anything about the critical need for knowledge and aware-ness? Have we learned anything about the importance of a relationship with God?

The Hecks, the McGowans, and "Ham" Mario Tyzbir can vividly recall the flaming debris, the columns of fire, the panic and pandemonium, the anguished cries of the dying. Newspaper accounts that have continued about the crash, the survivors.

It is as if we are still searching for the lesson.

The search for the lessons of Tenerife goes on at many levels. Tower control people will see the need to speak in clear terms and demand clear replies. Government agencies, pressed from all sides, will see the need to give air safety a higher priority.

Aircraft manufacturers, faced with the subtle decision of spending still more for safety—balancing the cost against the increment of improvement—will permit the scale balance to favor human safety.

One such device is a safety system that prevents fuel tank explosions. It has been used by the U.S. Air Force for more than 15 years successfully. New and less combustible materials for the aircraft interior, and cutting back on the acrid smoke which plagued us all. These could have prevented countless deaths in the Tenerife crash, according to engineer Bill Brookley of Wright-Patterson Air Force Base, one of those responsible for the development of improved safety systems.

The fuel tank system works by replacing the air in the empty space in the fuel tanks with nitrogen. An inert gas, nitrogen prevents combustion. It prevents fire and explosion due to electrical equipment sparks, lightning, or the friction sparks such as in the Tenerife crash.

Hundreds of lives might have been saved had this equipment been installed in all large jets since the FAA recommended it. In fact, the FAA report noted that the ignition of vapors in fuel tanks had been responsible for five accidents prior to 1970 that took 291 lives.

The immediate spread of fire in our Pan Am plane had to be due to burning fuel. The safety device would not have prevented that. But it might have prevented some of the explosions. There were two explosions while I was in the plane. Two more after I left. Some of these may have been fuel tanks exploding.

Explosion rocked the KLM plane and burned all within that plane. Might there have been some survivors if the tanks had been so equipped? These new systems would have added much weight and cost. Air travel is safe travel. But safety must be an ongoing fight. Airlines will be goaded by experiences like Tenerife. Safer air travel will be a consequence.

The repercussions of Tenerife will continue to spread like ever-widening ripples in a lake. Some will be negative:

• There may be people in Holland who lost their loved ones and who may themselves never fly because of that.

• There may be families of the Pan Am dead who may be similarly affected.

• There may be persons who have had their sense of religion shaken by the wholesale slaughter of young and old alike, without seeming rhyme or reason. They will have blamed God for man's folly.

• There may be young women who decide not to become stewardesses, and young men who decide not to go to flying school.

• There may be survivors who permit their minds to dwell on the screams, the burning flesh, the moans, the sight of a burned corpse or a morgue holding the mother and her child.

• There may be nightmares, bereavement, and scarring.

• There may be volunteers who will become soured on volunteering.

• There may be medical people who work in burn clinics who will want to change their specialty.

As Dr. Berthold Schwarz, a New Jersey psychiatrist, put it, "For many, it will be a lifetime of nightmares, fear of flying, fear for their loved ones during times of separation. And then there will be the guilt: Why did others die and not me? The phobias, the deep depression—these things can come."

One sound that Harold McGowan keeps hearing is a woman, amid the flames, screaming for help, with no possible way to reach her. How long will it ring in his ears?

Several survivors froze at the sight of the plane waiting in Las Palmas to fly them back to the United States. How long will the sight of a big plane waiting for them to board send chills up and down their flesh?

One question that plagues Edward Lamp of Walnut Creek, California is, "You ask yourself, why, why, why? And there's no answer." How long will this question go un-answered and continue to torture him?

Caroline Hopkins of Northbrook, Illinois, recovering physically with her husband, Warren, is still feeling other kinds of scars. "People talk to me and I'm not listening. I suddenly lapse into silence, not seeing, not talking." Even her sleep is interrupted by the returning sights and sounds. "I wake up in the middle of the night and there it is in front of me." In time it will go, but when?

For each survivor, the Tenerife tragedy is becoming more and more distant in time with every passing day.

"We're happy. Yes. And we're lucky."

These positive words spoken by Warren Hopkins are mere whisperings in the cacophonic din of disaster.

"I would have perished if God hadn't helped me escape. And without His help, I couldn't face the memory of it day after day. You can't sleep in the first days, but now I pray a lot and that helps."

These positive words, spoken by Floy Heck, are like the tinkle of wind chimes in the roar of a tornado.

A drive for more efficiency and safety by airline personnel—"Building an airline of KLM's standing requires a special kind of dedication. Like matching a point of being punctual. A quality that is very much a part of the Dutch. . . . That similar Dutch ability for doing things well. As you'll discover when you fly KLM. You'll find your trust sincerely reciprocated. With efficiency, punctualness and friendly understanding. For that is the way the people of Holland are."

After the wreck, the efficient Dutch hearts must have sunk. How unaware now of time the punctual Dutch dead.

Norman Williams and
George Otis during
High Adventure television show.

CHAPTER ELEVEN
Second Chance

My mother and I talked about my future plans. How could I share "Miracles of Rescue"? I somehow knew I might not have to wait too long.

"I owe my life to God's Word." Such phrases now came quite easily. Whereas a couple of months before I would have said what I wanted to say in more "diplomatic" or roundabout ways, not wanting to come on too strong.

But now I wanted to come on strong—to tell it like it is.

Then I met George Otis. He is a writer and a television personality. The first night we met, George invited me to guest on his nationally-syndicated television show "High Adventure."

I would be pretty much at the mercy of his questions and the way he reacted to my answers. I remembered the brusqueness of the reporters at Tenerife, their insensitivity to some they were interviewing. But George Otis didn't strike me as the usual reporter. When I described him to Mother, she remarked, "He might be the answer to our prayer."

My "High Adventure" TV appearance lasted only half an hour. It came off well. George Otis went at the story hard but threw no curves, offered me no stumbling blocks to trip on. I was both relieved and exhilarated at the sparkle of the show. We had chatted before the taping and I found he was not just seeking sensationalism. His interests were similar to mine. We were a good team. After the show, George spoke, "You must write a book, Norman. The story behind the story needs to be heard." I told him I wasn't a writer, that I could speak a little but I certainly couldn't write. But he was persistent. "A book will reach those you can never reach in person. Furthermore," George said, "this is a golden opportunity to squash a cruel myth. Careless people have a tendency to blame God for every kind of a disaster. Even the insurance companies label them 'Acts of God.' It is time to lift God from the unfair role of being a villain in every crisis and let Him be seen in His true role as a rescuer of the victims of catastrophe."

I still protested. But my defenses were crumbling. The idea of writing a book had never occurred to me. It seemed as out of place at that moment as a pair of roller skates and me here on crutches.

George sat opposite me at a table. His chin rested in his cupped hands. Suddenly he straightened up. "I'll write your book. It is a must story. It is straining to be told." He paused. "We'll call it *Terror at Tenerife.*"

George's enthusiasm was infectious. In a few minutes I, too, was "seeing a book."

On the third of May we flew off to Hawaii to get it started. Overlooking the green waters and blue skies of Waikiki, we sat down with George's friend, Bob Stone, and started to tape my recollections. At first it went haltingly, it was coming hard. Then suddenly it started. My memories flooded back.

God was moving me again.

When I got back from the short trip to Hawaii there were a flood of invitations for me to speak. Now the chips were down. But could I deliver before an audience?

This was the field I was trained in a quarter century ago. So long ago. Was I getting a second chance?

I stood a bit shakily and started to speak:

"In crisis the person without God in his life cries, 'Help!' The Christian cries, 'Jesus!'

"The terror at Tenerife from which I walked away practically unscathed seemed a clear-cut message to me.

"That message says, 'Norman Williams, you have led people on half the trip with business training for this life. Now you must lead them along the other half for their eternity.'

"I read Isaiah 43 which had taken on new meaning inside the dying Pan Am plane. 'When thou walkest through the fire, thou shalt not be burned; neither shall the flame kindle upon thee for I am the Lord thy God, . . . thy Savior.' "

"Nobody on that plane or KLM was planning on dying that day.

"Are you planning?

"Eternal life belongs to you, if you want. It's just a matter of whether you are going to accept, or reject it.

"Be prepared. When things like this happen—when this tremendous 747 plowed into the plane it was too late to think about the sinner's prayer."

Then I told about the cloud on the Peak of Hell at Tenerife and how it descended from the mountain as I watched it and we sat there "socked in." And about the strange concoction of people and how they reminded me of *Ship of Fools*, with passengers that were already dead and did not know it. And when I had spoken to Ted, "Ted, I don't know what you and I are doing here. Many are sailing into eternity and don't know it." The last words exchanged by me and my associate. . . . Then the normal warning, "Fasten your seat belts." We were moving, taxiing . . . then, the lurch to the left. The tremendous crash. Explosion! Inferno! Instant fire! Instant hell or instant heaven? . . . The strength of that prayer with my mother bringing down an anointing of the Holy Spirit in crisis. . . .

"In the name of Jesus and through Your shed blood, I

stand upon Your Word! I stand upon Your Word!" I broke down telling this point. Tears came and my voice cracked. Strength returned. "It was the Holy Spirit who gave me strength to ward off white hot flying debris. . . . " I spoke on. "If the Lord had required me to die at that moment, I would have gone with the same joyous feeling. Now I knew . . . I don't think I'll ever again be afraid. Like I have been born-again, again. Everyone has questions about how we are going to die. We just don't know. But this is the believer's extra edge. Death has lost its sting."

Why, I was preaching again!

"Born again—again." It sounds trite and melodramatic, but those are the only words to describe the feeling. The same feeling I had while being driven to the Tenerife waiting room.

Another chance in life. What shall I do with it?

Were other survivors experiencing the same feeling? Were they, too, exhilarated? Elevated? Reborn?

And now, through Christ, all the kindness of God has been poured out upon us . . . and now he is sending us around the world to tell all people everywhere the great things God has done for them, so they too, will believe and obey him.
(Romans 1, *TLB*)

A very personal catastrophe.

Photo: Henri Bureau/Sygma

CHAPTER TWELVE
Future Shock

An earthquake hits a Central American city. It is destroyed. The people gird for a great effort. They rebuild their city better than it was before. A typhoon levels Guam. A string of tornadoes wreck havoc in Texas. A tidal wave destroys a town in Hawaii. In each case human strength is challenged and the dust of disaster forms the foundation for bigger and better things.

How about Tenerife? What can be made better?

Out of the darkness of those memories, those fears, and those nightmares, what light can shine?

It would be egotistical to think that I can shine as much as that light.

God's light not mine.

It would also be totally thankless of me to walk away from Tenerife into a business-as-usual life. I would be ignoring an experience that could send its positive ripples out in ever-widening circles.

I am thankful.

But I have memories, too. The searing flames I remember in terms of my unsinged hair. The screams of the dying I remember in terms of my life. The pools of blood I remember in terms of Jesus' shed blood.

I remember people like Grace Ellerbrock of Laguna

Beach, seated next to me in the C-141, her husband suffering from a broken pelvis in a stretcher just a few feet in front of us. "I was able to pull him along the ground until we were a safe distance from the wreckage," she recalled. "I could not do this. I am not strong enough. An unusual strength became mine." A great lady!

When I remember people's actions . . . The Tenerife people mourning the dead. The angel of mercy who boarded the plane in San Antonio, a volunteer who swept among the passengers doing what she could to make us comfortable, bringing water and coffee and arranging a seat so that I might lift my painful foot.

The victims. I remember the victim who was my colleague. I remember his energies, his abilities, his ambitions, and zest for life. I remember his love of his wife and his plans for his three young sons. His mother and father and sister and their grief.

Kinds of memories of a happy reunion lasting for years to come. They will outlive and outshine the dark aspects of Tenerife.

Even letting my feet hang down the side of the bed and pulling up my breakfast tray to eat in a normal position was a welcome beginning of that freedom, as was shaving, bathing, and taking care of my personal needs without my tractioned foot up in the air and an attendant to help me.

But "true" mobility began on Thursday, April 6. I was taken for my first experience with crutches. I put these two sticks under my armpits and attempted to move. I tried and tried. Perspiration flowed. I was able to take my first step.

"Great!" encouraged one of the attendants. "You've got it!"

I was glad that he thought so. I never worked so hard to move 18 inches.

"I'm not much of a swinger," I said.

More shaking, perspiring and waddling. I felt like an 85-year-old. In 10 minutes I was back in bed.

On my 52nd birthday, I was back in therapy, grunting and heaving. After that third day, I had the knack. I felt I could master those babies after all. I could waddle along on those aluminum legs. I would even go up and down stairs with them.

In that cast, I was free—free to shine the light of our Savior into the shadows of the Peak of Hell.

There were tears in my eyes when they rolled into my room the bed of Mrs. Kay Sinnett of Longview, Washington. Her husband Dick was still recuperating from burns in another division of the hospital. She had broken both ankles jumping from the wing.

"I heard you were leaving. Lucky you," she said. "I wanted to say good-bye." She smiled radiantly.

What a closeness you feel. It was as if she were a member of the family.

"God be with you and Dick. I know you both will be quickly healed and leaving for home soon, also," were my words to her.

They wheeled her out and brought in a wheelchair to take me to my waiting car. In my hands I held those two aluminum sticks. I gripped them firmly, knowing they would be my "mobility" in the weeks ahead.

Moving out into the California sunshine, I was again moved to tears.

Arriving home again, I was impressed with the comforts in the house. They all seemed so new to me. A fresh gulp of life?

My little dog El Toro was happy to see me but a bit confused by my two extra "legs."

I developed a new appreciation of people's concern for the handicapped, and, a much greater understanding of their problems.

People really want to give of themselves. Offered the chance, they do so spontaneously and unselfishly. They were so good to us. People are the treasure of the world.

Tears came to my eyes when I began driving my car on April 10—Easter Sunday. Need I say why?

As a handicapped driver I became aware of those parking spaces marked and reserved for the handicapped. I used to resent them. Now I respect their availability.

Tears. Moist eyes. And more tears.

Tears of love for the Lord. But tears were not enough.

Soon I traveled by crutch and by wheelchair, but off I went to radio shows, television shows, church meetings, and taping that book in Hawaii.

God has taken me at my word. There have been listening ears.

However, there are ears and eyes that I especially long to touch—*yours.* Oh, that I might be a poet with such eloquence I could reach all. While there is yet time—before the curtain of this life drops.

If you do say "yes" to Him, you'll be heading for a real eternity where everything turns up roses.

Now for one final glance back on Tenerife. The story of Erma Schlecht and her real-life roses. . . .

The engines kept running.

Photo: Henri Bureau — Agence Sygma

CHAPTER THIRTEEN
Everything Coming up Roses

People were broken and burned in the crash. Few got off like me without a hair singed. Still there were triumphs and miracles galore. Erma Schlecht is a walking miracle herself.

Erma says, "I leaned back catnapping . . . dozing on and off. Just waiting for this dragged-out flight to leave Tenerife. So wonderful to know I was here in God's will. I thought back on all the difficulties of getting my passport. Finally I had prayed, "OK, Lord, if You want me to go on this cruise, You will have to work it out.' He did!

"I was thinking it had been a good flight—I'd met some nice people. I glanced down at the box of pink roses Carlette Reynolds had given me when I left my Longview, Washington home that morning. When we get to the ship, I decided, I'd give two roses to my new friends, Mr. and Mrs. Charles Miller, in Seats 35B and 35C beside me. I was still glowing from the opportunity I got on the flight over to talk to them about Christ. They had so graciously listened, very moved.

"My friends, Hal and Pat Branscome, had also given me a beautiful rose corsage. I had changed to my long-sleeved blouse, polka dot vest and pantsuit to show off the corsage. It later proved to be providential that I had changed from the sleeveless outfit.

"Captain Grubbs' voice came over the P.A. system,

'Please extinguish your cigarettes, fasten your seat belts. KLM is finally moving. We will be rolling out momentarily.'

"I must have dozed again from the gentle rocking of the taxiing airliner.

"Suddenly I was wide awake! The plane went into convulsions. Up, down, sideways, with horrible tearing sounds. I felt searing pains from fire—smoke, explosions—everything was going black.

"I remember putting my hands over my face and saying an unusual thing, 'Lord, today I will see You.' Immediately a draft of the most beautiful air hit me—just before I had been choking for oxygen. Now the sweetest air I had ever breathed.

"I opened my eyes and saw skin hanging from my hands. I looked around for that heavenly air and found it. A jagged hole way in front. I talked to my roses, 'You'll have to stay, I can't take you.'

"Black smoke and fire swirled at me again. The Millers were out in the aisle. Something said, 'Don't get in anyone's way in the aisles!' So I unfastened my belt, put my flight bag over my shoulder, then with effortless moves I leaped over the seat in front of me. How did I do that? . . .

"Then I sprang over two more rows of seats. The breathable air and a light beckoned me toward some kind of an opening. It was like the Lord was saying, 'Come this way, come this way,' and He was leading me. Hadn't He written, 'My God will enlighten my darkness . . . By my God have I leaped over a wall' (Psalm 18).

"When I got near the jagged hole I fought my way through the fire and wreckage until I was out on the wing. It was so slippery with oil. No one was around so I sat down and slid toward a 30-foot drop. But I landed right in burning debris. How thankful I had changed to my long-sleeved blouse. It protected me from that horrible fire I had fallen right into!

"I jumped up and scrambled away from the exploding

plane. Finally I reached some cool, cool moist grass. I gently placed my seared hands deep into it. It momentarily relieved some of the pain. I glanced down: 'Oh, my beautiful rose corsage is gone! I lost it in the escape. How sad.'

"I sat there watching the death of our plane and prayed, 'Oh, Lord, I've made it. Oh, please help the rest of them.'

"A van drove up and a man loaded the wounded inside. He had left the front door open so I crawled in next to the driver's seat under my own power. We sped off to the hospital.

"After awhile the nurses brought another survivor into my room. It turned out to be Floy Heck.

"Floy looked over at me observantly, then asked, 'Are you a Christian?'

"I said, 'Why yes, are you?'

"Right then we had a prayer meeting.

"Later I talked to Floy about my need for God to give me an emotional healing. We prayed together. I dozed off and slept like a baby. From that time to this I have never had another incident of terror or nightmares. I was healed! Prayer was my salvation from disaster and a sure-fire medicine now for my bruised emotions.

"The next day Anthony Giordano, a missionary, came in to pray with us. He asked, 'Erma, do you have a message for anyone?' My answer came out without thinking, 'Oh yes, please go and tell all our dear survivors that "Today is the day of salvation." '

"When my daughter Diane heard the news of my rescue she said, 'I knew no matter what, Mom is a Christian. And if she didn't make it, then she's in Heaven with Dad.'

"As we boarded the plane to return home two men came running. One was the driver of the van. He was returning the flight bag I had lost in the shuffle. Can you imagine me carrying that out of the wreck?

"The other was Anthony Giordano. He called out at me, 'Erma, I have good news for you. I gave your message to the survivors. The harvest was beautiful!'

"For some, God was turning the remnants of disaster to glory. A phoenix from the ashes of Tenerife."

> Glory be to God who by his mighty power at work within us is able to do far more than we would ever dare to ask or even dream of—infinitely beyond our highest prayers, desires, thoughts, or hopes. (Ephesian 3, *TLB*)

Erma Schlecht,
"The rose lady"
Longview, Washington

CHAPTER FOURTEEN
In Memoriam

So many brave, so many kind, so many dear. The legacies of Tenerife are sweet memories of those who loved the perished and the injured. In both the writing and the reading of this book we too have come "to know" the people on both those craft . . . and we too have come to love.

Shortly after the accident Pan American officials graciously released a list of those on board Clipper "Victor." There are two things we must remember in the reading of it. Since then there have been certain "changes of status." Secondly, under the circumstances, it would not be unlikely that some errors exist. Please forgive.

We hereby present this "HONOR ROLL" as a memorial to each on board the airliners.

The KLM list was unavailable at the time of writing, but let us make this crystal clear. There is no question about the caliber of precious human cargo aboard Captain van Zanten's "The Rhine." He was a pilot's pilot and an airman with a superb record. From the perspective of eternity we shall hear tales of great heroism which also took place "down the runway" in the dying KLM.

☆ ☆ ☆ ☆ ☆

List of known survivors of the Pan America 747 involved in the Canary Islands crash, as provided by Pan Am officials:

Amador, John; Marina del Rey
Andersen, Marion; San Diego
Anderson, Dr. Karen; Seattle
Bowman, Richard; El Cerrito, Calif.
Bowman, Mary; El Cerrito, Calif.
Brown, Jan; Laguna Hills
Brusco, Cleo; Lake Oswego, Ore.
Brusco, Roland; Longview, Wash.
Brusco, Teresa; Longview, Wash.
Combs, John; Haleiwa, Hawaii
Combs, Louise; Haleiwa, Hawaii
Culbertson, Stephen; Green Valley Ariz.
Culbertson, Ruth; Green Valley, Ariz.
Daniel, Patricia; La Verne
Daniel, Lynda; La Verne
Ellerbrock, Byron; Laguna Hills
Ellerbrock, Grace; Laguna Hills
Fox, Kim; Visalia, Calif.
Heck, Paul; Laguna Hills
Holt, Joan Devereau; San Diego
Hess, Edward; Phoenix
Hopkins, Warren; Northbrook, Ill.
Hopkins, Caroline; Northbrook, Ill.
Jakoubek, Marianne; Visalia, Calif.
Kershaw, Dorthea; Borrego Springs, Calif.
Lamp, Edward; Walnut Creek, Calif.
Libert, Alta; Hemet
Lord, Ms. Isabelle; Long Beach (author's note: Ms. Lord died
    en route home)
Magante, Maurice; Sacramento
McGowan, Harold; Laguna Hills
McGowan, Mrs. Grace; Laguna Hills
Miller, Charles; Escondido
Monde, Anthony; La Mesa
Monde, Mrs. Isobel; La Mesa
Moore, Mrs. Bethene, San Francisco
Naik, Jim; Cupertino, Calif.

Naik, Mrs. Elfreida; Cupertino, Calif.
Pinkstaff, Charles; San Diego
Reynolds, Bennett; San Leandro, Calif.
Reynolds, Mrs. Madeline; San Leandro, Calif.
Rich, Mrs. Pamela; Woodlake, Calif.
Ridout, Edgar; Alpine, Calif.
Schlecht, Erma; Palm Springs (author's note: Erma's home is
    Longview, Wash.)
Simon, Mrs. Ethel; Los Angeles
Sinnett, Richard; Longview, Wash.
Sinnett, Mrs. Kay; Longview, Wash.
Sparacino, S.; Medford, Ore.
Tanemura, Roy; Kelowna, B.C.
Tartikoff, Jordan; San Francisco
Tartikoff, Mrs. Enid; San Francisco
Trumbull, Col. Albert; La Mesa, Calif.
Trumbull, Mrs. Florence; La Mesa, Calif.
Tyzbir, Mario; Laguna Hills
Waldrip, Herbert; Laguna Hills
Waldrip, Lara; Laguna Hills
Walker, Larry; Laguna Hills
Walker, Phyllis; Laguna Hills
Waters, Col. Mervin; Petaluma, Calif. (author's note: died in
    Tenerife hospital)
Wiley, David; Palo Alto
Williams, Norman; Palos Verdes
Heck, Floy; Laguna Hills

Crew members surviving:

Grubbs, Victor, captain; Centerport, N.Y.
Bragg, Robert, first officer, Howard Beach, N.Y.
Warns, George, flight engineer; Blairstown, N.Y.
Kelly, Dorothy, purser; New Hampshire
Jackson, Joan, flight attendant; Nashville
Johnson, Carla, flight attendant; New York City
Donovan, Susanne, flight attendant; Harrisburg Pa.

List of Pan American passengers who were killed in the Canary Island crash, as provided by Pan Am officials:

Achatz, Wilma; Washington
Adams, Louise; Whittier
Adams, Wilton; San Marino
Adams, Edna; San Marino
Ames, Helen; Anaheim
Anderson, Leondre; San Diego
Anderson, Carl; San Diego
Anderson, Margaret; San Diego
Araujo, Rhelma; Oakland
Aston, Frank; Hemet
Aston, Marie; Hemet
Axford, Duncan; Scottsdale, Ariz.
Axford, Arlene; Scottsdale, Ariz.
Bailey, William; Moreland, Ohio
Bailey, Naomi; Moreland, Ohio
Baldwin, Charlotte; Washington, D.C.
Barkdull, James; San Diego
Barkdull, Alice; San Diego
Babron, Richard; San Pedro
Barth, Fred; Escondido
Barth, Kathryn; Escondido
Bartholhew, Esther; Long Beach
Basickowski, James; Los Angeles
Beards, Ann; Ely, Nev.
Beardslee, Mabel; Rosemead
Bebee, Hazel; Montclair, Calif.
Bellah, Sara; Whittier
Bellah, Hazel; Whittier
Belluokini, Fred; Sacramento
Belluokini, Iva; Sacramento
Bernascowi, Remy; Redwood City, Calif.
Bernascowi, Iena; Redwood City, Calif.
Berne, George; Redwood City, Calif.

Berne, Helen; Redwood City, Calif.

Beutel, Fred; Pasadena

Blackburn, Fay; Long Beach

Blanche, Ethel; Laguna Hills

Bock, Anita; Chimacun, Wash.

Robinson, Marge; Incline Village, Nev. This name is also
reported as being spelled Bodison.

Bolles, Edward; Honolulu

Bolles, Jeanette; Honolulu

Boyington, Carol; Watsonville, Calif.

Bradley, Col. Clifford; San Juan Capistrano

Bradley, Marjorie; San Juan Capistrano

Brandenberg, Brita; Corona del Mar

Brassfield, Mable; Laguna Hill

Briggs, Jessie, Del Mar

Brown, Carlyle; Vancouver, Wash.

Brown, Elizabeth; Vancouver, Wash.

Calandra, James; Fresno

Calandra, Irma; Fresno

Campbell, Henry; Davis, Calif.

Campbell, Helen; Davis, Calif.

Caza, Elizabeth; Windsor, Ont.

Chatterton, Lloyd; Laguna Hills

Chatterton, Helen; Laguna Hills

Chounet, Anna; Watsonville, Calif.

Church, Elsie; Studio City

Cochran, Myra; Laguna Hills

Cocke, James; Watsonville, Calif.

Cohen, Stanley; San Diego

Cohen, Helen; San Diego

Collis, Langley; Stockton

Collis, Mrs. Langley; Stockton

Combs, William; Laguna Hills

Combs, Leone; Laguna Hills

Cornell, Milton; Orange

Cox, Wilbur; San Jose, Calif.

Cox, La Welle; San Jose
Craig, Oliver; Longview, Wash.
Craig, Mildred; Longview, Wash.
Crawford, Kenneth; San Diego
Crawford, Ruth; San Diego
Crosby, Eleanor; Oroville, Calif.
Culver, Emily; West St. Paul, Minn.
Daniel, Jack; La Verne
Dimnock, Russell; Beverly Hills
Dinwiddie, Hardaway; Phoenix
Dinwiddie, Loraine; Phoenix
Donald, Lillian; San Diego
Dordich, Roy; San Jose
Dordich, Katherine; San Jose
Dordich, Stephan; San Jose
Edelman, Walter; La Jolla, Calif.
Cornelius, D.; Woodland Hills
Cornelius, Mrs. D.; Woodland Hills
Edmunds, Merritt; Oceanside
Edmunds, Marjorie; Oceanside
Efird, Dr. Robert; Seattle
Ellis, Catherine; Pinedale, Calif.
Ellsworth, Sherman; Laguna Hills
Ellsworth, Marian; Laguna Hills
Emerzian, Philip; Mill Valley, Calif.
Ensminger, Philip; Beverly Hills
Evans, Raymond; San Diego
Evans, Hallie; San Diego
Fisher, Martin; Laguna Hills
Fitzgerald, George; Santa Cruz, Calif.
Foley, Genevieve; Palos Verdes
Fox, Margaret; Visalia, Calif.
Freedman, Emily; Daly City, Calif.
Frier, Esther; Orange
Fyr, Robert; El Paso
Fyr, Mrs. Francis; El Paso

Gardner, Lucille; Las Vegas, Nev.

Garner, Mildred; Ogden, Utah

Geiberger, Ray; Santa Barbara

Gilson, Margaret; Glendale

Godfrey, Emilie; Coronado

Guedhart, Robert; Newport Beach

Guedhart, Beverly; Newport Beach

Grimwood, Maurine; Emeryville, Calif.

Grupp, Herbert; San Diego

Grupp, Mrs. Herbert; San Diego

Guerriero, Domenick; Fresno

Guerriero, Elizabeth; Fresno

Jakoubek, Robert; Visalia, Calif.

Jeans, Joseph; Albany, Calif.

Halldorson, Raymond; Laguna Hills

Halldorson, Helen; Laguna Hills

Hamann, Peter; San Jose

Hamann, Frances; San Jose

Hammond, Frances; Peoria, Ill.

Harlow, Jeanne; Las Vegas, Nev.

Harmon, Bernice; Rancho Mirage, Calif.

Harper, Howard; Marina Del Rey

Hart, Jane; La Jolla, Calif.

Hauser, Art; San Diego

Hauser, Helen; San Diego

Hegdahl, Col. Rudolph; San Diego

Hegdahl, Lucille; San Diego

Hempel, Mignonne; Boulder Creek, Calif.

Hempel, William; Boulder Creek, Calif.

Henning, Hans; Langley, Wash.

Henning, Elly; Langley, Wash.

Herb, Alfred; San Diego

Herb, Eileen; San Diego

Hess, Mary; Phoenix. A family friend says he talked with her
    husband, who survived the crash, and quotes the
    husband as saying Mrs. Hess also is alive.

Hicks, Clara; hometown unavailable
Hirshfield, Matile; Long Beach
Hirschfield, Matile; Long Beach
Hohner, Vera; Santa Ana
Houston, Jean; Laguna Hills
Hoyt, John, Incline Village, Nev.
Huffman, Clarence; Riverside
Huffman, Gloria; Riverside
Jeans, Martha; Albany, Calif.
Johnson, Bev; Grants Pass, Ore.
Johnson, Paul; Los Angeles
Johnson, Madeline; Los Angeles
Johnson, Perry, Santa Monica
Johnson, Mrs. Perry; Santa Monica
Johnson, Monica; Santa Monica
Johnson, Lisa; Santa Monica
Johnston, Dorothy; Escondido
Johnston, Monte; Newport Beach
Johnston, Patricia; Newport Beach
Jordan, Gertrude; Los Angeles
Kase, Frank; Laguna Hills
Kase, Gwendolyn; Laguna Hills
Keller, Idalee; Ogden, Utah
Kershaw, Frank; Borrego Springs, Calif.
Kirkorian, Gloria; Palm Desert
Knox, Robert; Rolling Hills.
Knox, Geraldine; Rolling Hills
Koslosky, Ralph; Anchorage
Koslosky, Ruby; Anchorage
Lamb, Linda; Watsonville, Calif.
Lamp, Nancy; Walnut Creek, Calif.
Lane, Gail; San Francisco
Langhorn, Nancy; Littleton, Colo.
Larsen, Leif; Langley, Wash.
Larsen, Elizabeth; Langley, Wash.
Larson, Karl; Laguna Hills

Larson, Lorraine; Laguna Hills
Lendl, Lydia; Torrance
Lewis, Jerry; Los Angeles
Lewis, Lila; Los Angeles
Libert, Maurice; Hemet
Lippmann, Alexander; La Jolla, Calif.
Lippmann, Evelyn; La Jolla, Calif.
Lively, Roscoe; Watsonville, Calif.
Locke, Donald; Long Beach.
Locke, Mrs. Donald; Long Beach
Magante, Cynthia; Sacramento
Malin, Benjamin; Laguna Hills
Marsden, Dorothy; Pasadena
McClintock, Myrtle; Los Altos, Calif.
McCullough, Gertrude; Santa Barbara
McPartland, Marty; Dallas
McRae, Frances; Santa Cruz, Calif.
Meyer, Eve; Hollywood
Miller, Dorothy; Escondido
Miller, A. W.; Phoenix
Miller, Mrs. A. W.; Phoenix
Mitchell, Walter; Kelowna B.C.
Mitchell, Evonne; Kelowna B.C.
Mitchell, Barbara; Bakersfield
Monty, William; Aptos, Calif.
Monty, Mary; Aptos, Calif.
Moore, Walter; San Francisco
Moran, Richard; Los Angeles
Moran, Dorothy; Los Angeles
Morris, Clifford; Burbank
Morris, Emilie, Burbank
Mueller, Richard; Long Beach
Mueller, Ruby; Long Beach
Murdock, Shirley; Long Beach
Nelson, Ben; San Mateo, Calif.
Nelson, Karin; San Mateo, Calif.

Nelson, Florence; Santa Barbara
Paris, Fred; Sepulveda
Paris, Roberta; Sepulveda
Parker, Robert; Capistrano Beach
Parker, Isabella; Capistrano Beach
Parkinon, Marietta; Oakland
Perry, Melva; La Jolla, Calif.
Peters, Helen; Laguna Hills
Pinkstaff, Mrs. Charles; San Diego
Pitcock, Genevieve; Sacramento
Querantes, Alvera; Redwood City, Calif.
Rasch, Robert; San Jose
Rasch, Doris; San Jose
Reed, Charles; Santa Ana
Reed, Lorraine; Santa Ana
Reed, Hazel; Escondido
Reed, Audrey; Ogden, Utah
Rehbock, Sara; Los Angeles
Reid, Norman; Lafayette, Calif.
Retling, Helen; Eugene, Ore.
Reining, Elizabeth; Laguna Hills
Reiter, Joseph; Los Altos, Calif.
Reiter, Glovif; Los Altos, Calif.
Robertson, Renee; Littleton, Colo.
Robertson, Marie; Fullerton
Roberts, Albert; Chino
Roberts, Albert; Chino
Roberts, Mrs. Verne; Chino
Roman, Ruth; Los Altos, Calif.
Rothstein, Milton; Los Angeles
Rothstein, Natallye; Los Angeles
Ruppell, Florence; Glendale, Ariz.
Saygol, Charles; Torrance
Soyous, Linda; Palm Springs
Seacrist, Katherine; Lahaina, Hawaii
Selbo, Ethel; Laguna Hills

Shapro, Alvin; Los Altos, Calif.
Shapro, Lillian; Los Altos, Calif.
Shaw, Beth; Rancho Santa Fe, Calif.
Shulkino, Aubrey; San Diego
Shulkino, Sylvia; San Diego
Shute, Lorelle; Fresno
Sibley, Richard; Fresno
Sibley, Mrs. Richard; Fresno
Silva, Frank; Redondo Beach
Silva, Mrs. Frank; Redondo Beach
Simmons, Francis; Laguna Hills
Simmons, Kathryn; Laguna Hills
Simon, Meyer, Los Angeles
Singleton, David; Bakersfield
Smith, Wilbur; Santa Ana
Smith, Mary Jane; Santa Ana
Smith, Mrs. Le Von; Ogden, Utah
South, William; Medford, Ore.
South, Judy; Medford, Ore.
Sparacino, Mrs. S.; Medford, Ore. This passenger is also
    reported to come from San Jose
Sparr, Florence; Laguna Hills
Spomer, Pat; Mill Valley, Calif.
Stebben, Michael; Santa Rosa, Calif.
Stebben, Arlene; Santa Rosa, Calif.
Stecher, Dennis; Santa Ana
Stecher, Margaret; Santa Ana
Steffarud, Byron; Phoenix
Steffarud, Goldie; Phoenix
Stevenson, Robert; San Clemente
Stevenson, Ann; San Clemente
Strandt, Betty; Glendale
Stringfellow, Joseph; Piedmont, Calif.
Stringfellow, Marlive; Piedmont, Calif.
Stuart, Helen; Crescent City, Calif.
Tanemura, Aya; Kelowna, B.C.

Taylor, Chalmer; San Diego
Taylor, Aenid; San Diego
Thomas, Emma; San Mateo, Calif.
Torres, Julio; Long Beach
Torres, Dora; Long Beach
Tyler, Maurice; San Diego
Tyler, Virginia; San Diego
Tyzbir, Irene; Laguna Hills
Van Resselaer, Eleanor; Santa Cruz, Calif.
Vedder, Walter; San Diego
Vedder, Irene; San Diego
Veglia, Albert; Sacramento
Veglia, Mary; Sacramento
Vernon, Helen; Laguna Hills
Vogel, Roy; Santa Barbara
Wallace, Harold; Los Angeles
Waltz, Charlotte; Reno, Nev.
Waters, Moreen; Petaluma, Calif.
Webber, Robert; Irvine
Webber, Mary; Irvine
Waldorf, David; New York
Weller, William; Chino
Weller, Hazel; Chino
White, Martha; Riverside
White, David; New York
Wilkinson, Joan; San Jose
Yee, S. (male), Foster City, Calif.
Yee, S. (female), Foster City, Calif.
Younes, Theodore, Palos Verdes
Ziebell, Charles; Laguna Hills
Ziebell, Fern; Laguna Hills
Moss, Beau; c-o Royal Cruise
Deliyantis, Tony; c-o Royal Cruise
Daily, F.; Bellevue, Wash.

Dead crew members:
De Beaulieu, Francoise Colbert, purser; New York

Asai, Mari, flight attendant; New York
Hirano, Sachiko, flight attendant; New York
Luker, Marilyn, flight attendant; Philadelphia
Sarp, Aysel, flight attendant; Arlington, Va.
Ekelund, Christine, flight attendant, New York
Thomas, Carol, flight attendant; New York
Torrech, Miguel, flight attendant; New York
Flood, Luisa, flight attendant; New York

Americans on KLM Plane

The Dutch airline KLM identified *four Americans who were among the KLM passengers killed in the Canary Islands as:*

D. Gillis and Mrs. J. Gillis; Mrs. T. Twist and her 18-month-old baby, all of Rochester, N.Y.

If you have been blessed by this book, the author, George Otis, would like to hear from you. Mr. Otis is an internationally known conference speaker, a prolific writer, book publisher and founder of "High Adventure" Ministries. This is a unique ministry reaching the government leaders and famous personalities of our day with the Gospel of Jesus Christ. If you would like to learn more about Mr. Otis and his ministry, write:

George Otis
c/o Omega Publications
P.O. Box 4130
Medford, OR 97501

Other books by George Otis:
MILLENNIUM MAN
CRISIS AMERICA
THE BLUEPRINT
HIGH ADVENTURE
PEACE, POWER AND HAPPINESS
GOD, MONEY AND YOU
THE GHOST OF HAGAR
ELDRIDGE CLEAVER: ICE AND FIRE!
THE THUNDER OF HIS POWER